P9-AFO-714

NEW SERIES • VOLUME XVIII

COSTERUS

Essays in
English and American
Language and Literature

1978

LYRICAL POSITIVISM

by

CARLEE LIPPMAN

© Editions Rodopi N.V., Amsterdam 1979
Printed in the Netherlands
ISBN: 90–6203–772–0

CONTENTS

C H A P T E R   I

SOME TENETS

i

It is difficult to talk about literature without creating
a myth about it. The myth results partly from the difference
in aim of literature and criticism, which is itself symbiotically
related to literature. A literary creation, qua creation, is
explicitly non-measurable. It lacks positive vertices, even
flees from them, retreating into a fuzzy area which is its chosen
domain. Any pretence that literature might make to "tell the
truth," to alert us to reality, is itself a lie. The less said
about literature's "verifiability," the better, the truer it
is to its gloriously irresponsible mission. Even "mission" is
too forthright a word here, too blandly an assumption that literature has any function at all. We can see the danger of a pur-
posive consciousness looking at its chosen object.

In writing even generally about literature, as we are doing, the pitfalls are glaring. We are trying, in our non-direct
way, to circumscribe literature with language, until it is bristling with adjectives not of its own choosing. At that stage,
after telling it repeatedly and in the most refined terms what
it is _not_, we tighten the noose. The critical circuit is completed; a light goes on in some obscure corner of the critic's
brain, and voilà, we have a myth, a pernicious myth, since we
have by now come to believe it ourselves. However careful we
try to be, there is no cure for this kind of spiral, which is,
it appears, self-sustaining.

The reader should by now have intuited the gross difference between literature and criticism. The one is trying to

say nothing, and the other to say something. Literature's entire privileged existence, conscious or otherwise, depends on
its freeing itself from the need to make sense, the need to be
internally coherent, the need to give discursive reasons for
its existence. Criticism only earns its bread if it can fill
in spaces, make intelligible, dominate with the weight of its
ratiocination. One can hardly deny the complementarity of this
relationship.

It is surprising how literature and criticism, in their
differentness, seem made for each other, in the romantic terms
of some old song. Can either be self-sufficient? Probably so,
but only to the extent that they violate their true natures.
Even mortal opposites in constant juxtaposition come in time
to resemble each other, however slight and superficial that
resemblance may be.

Two examples come to mind: the novel Rayuela by Julio
Cortázar and the critical study La distance intérieure by Georges
Poulet. In each we find criticism or literature attempting to
turn into its opposite. The Cortázar novel, known more famil-
iarly to English-speaking readers as Hopscotch, is a highly self-
conscious attempt to reduce the form of the novel to a series
of interchangeable episodes and then mix them up. To read the
book in its entirety, the reader is forced to hop around from
front to back, and to read many chapters that are rather technical literary criticism. Whether that criticism concerns itself with the episodic parts of Hopscotch or not is debatable,
but criticism's "intrusion" into literature is unquestionable.
(Its total assimilation is doubtful.)

In La distance intérieure, Poulet's conception of himself
as a creative artist is forced to the fore-front of our consciousness. That he seeks to present literature as a system of tensions, as his system of tensions, is undeniable. That literature is lifted bodily from its natural contexts, in the service

of this _idée fixe_, is also all too evident. Yet it is a masterly and compelling work, one which adds a certain depth to the way we look at the literary objects under discussion.

From just these two examples (obviously oversimplified to make a point), we see a tendency toward the convergence of literature and criticism. Each tries to include the other, and thereby neutralize it; each behaves like a bacteriophage engulfing bacteria. The potential for idiosyncrasy is in this way greatly reduced, differences leveled, and the resulting amalgam offered for sale on the marketplace, trimmed of all thorns.

Though in somewhat different form, the neutralization of criticism in this way is not an absolutely new idea. Eighteenth-century writers were terribly conscious of the ultimate judgments their literary offspring would undergo. People like Pope and Dryden always had a word for their dearly-beloved critics, fossilized for a time in Heroic Couplets. In this way the critics were reduced and found themselves contributing willy-nilly to the very meter and rhyme scheme of the product they so abhorred, their names and bodily characteristics lending it substance.

This example is admittedly an extension of the concept of "criticism" verging on literary biography, and of course, satire. The point is that critics and _littérateurs_ often find themselves in the same camp, if not in the same bed, because of essentially parallel preoccupations. But what if we look at a point of view which is, in its stated objectives, as hostile to aesthetic expression as anything in writing could be? This is the point of view of a group of writers variously called the language philosophers, language analysts, logical positivists, Vienna Circle. The attributions are numerous because the group is far-flung geographically and chronologically, spanning a period from 1890 to the present and having as its centers places as diverse as Germany, England, and the United States. (Not to mention the many other countries in which their thinking has seemed fertile.)

The prime seduction of the thinking of this philosophical enclave is the epistemologic certainty towards which their efforts are directed. To say clearly what one is thinking, and to know that such thought is correct and externally verifiable more or less sketches out the asserted (and often achieved) purpose of the group. To point at, and thereby isolate the pernicious tendencies of thought which does not share this sort of purposiveness is also an implicit part of their thinking.

Ideas as revered and insubstantial as notions about the existence of God or the reality of the external world are shown to be nothing more than grammatically correct but nonsensical expressions. And when large ideas like these meet their analytic end, one can imagine the sort of chaos occurring on the local level, the region of expression and concept. It is, in fact, on the basis of smaller cognitive units--like the sentence or proposition--that any larger ontological statement can be made. Given this obvious fact, the smaller units are also more vulnerable to attack. The house of cards falls with the removal of its lowest level.

In a way, this insistence on attention to the linguistic substratum of ideas was a useful purging of grandiose philosophical notions having no basis but the vehemence with which they were advanced by energetic philosophers. That language, in order to be an accurate picture of the world, must demonstrate an isomorphism with every fact it describes, is a simple concept with shattering ramifications. In these terms, talking about God as one would talk about a table, is illogical, since one is present to the senses, while the other usually, is not. Being able to point out or clearly formulate the object of a linguistic statement was a desideratum strongly insisted on by many of

the tougher-minded of the group, notably A. J. Ayer and R.
Carnap. What could be more damaging to literature than a requirement that every statement be directly verifiable in experience, or that one be able to point to a method that, if applied,
would validate the statement? This is Ayer's criterion for
meaning, and it is clear that such a requirement leaves a major-
ity of utterances floundering in a sea of senselessness, literature being one of the first victims.

There are a number of ways out of this impasse. One is
to say that literature is indeed without demonstrable meaning;
that is its prerogative. Another is that Language, Truth and
Logic[1] is a youthful book, and that many of the statements in
it were later modified by Ayer himself and other language
analysts. A third is to accept the criterion as a challenge,
a demand that literature examine itself and its methods, and
see whether it has (or desires) a claim for meaning, or whether
other criteria are more valuable to its full realization as a
man-made artifact. By the end of the book, we may be able to
decide which of these alternatives to accept.

A humorous addendum to the question of verifiability should
help put things into perspective. While we quake and tremble
at the rigor of Ayer's demand, we should be aware of the fact
that history has already taken its own revenge. On page thirty-
six of his book, Ayer gives an example of verifiability in principle:

> There remain a number of significant propositions,
> concerning matters of fact, which we could not
> verify even if we chose; simply because we lack
> the practical means of placing ourselves in the
> situation where the relevant observations could
> be made. A simple and familiar example of such

---

[1] A. J. Ayer, Language, Truth and Logic (New York 1936).

> a proposition is the proposition that there are
> mountains on the farther side of the moon. No
> rocket has yet been invented which would enable
> me to go and look at the farther side of the moon,
> so that I am unable to decide the matter by
> actual observation. But I do know what observa-
> tions would decide it for me, if as is theoreti-
> cally conceivable, I were once in a position to
> make them. And therefore I say that the proposi-
> tion is verifiable in principle, if not in prac-
> tice, and is accordingly significant.[2]

Even logic seems subject to history, at least in the examples
it chooses to demonstrate its laws. In this instance, although
the logical system doesn't exactly totter, the sensuous framework that it supports and which furnishes it with an object has
begun to erode. Time has blurred the sharp edges of a self-
justifying series of statements about reality as we perceive it.
And indeed, even Wittgenstein in his theoretical about-face from
the Tractatus to the Investigations, came to realize that the
external reality of statements about reality was not under discussion at all, merely the logic of grammar. What all this is
pointing toward is that even rather rigid systems like that of
Ayer are finally subject to whimsical events beyond their control, as vulnerable, that is, as literature to changing conditions. This is not meant as a serious objection to the logical
positivists, although it has been advanced by many. Our purpose
in this book is not to criticize the aims or methods of this
group of philosophers, but rather to raid them in an attempt
to see literature freshly.

In talking about the concerns of these philosophers, we
started with the question of verifiability, which is perhaps
on the outermost fringe of their thought. Not that accuracy isn't
an implicit part of the program, endemic to all thinking. But
there are issues that are less bristling with the immediate

---

[2]Ibid.

threat of external, empirical confirmation, questions that concern internal issues like language and the logic (or illogic)
of its applications for example. In the following pages I will
deal with those issues which seem most adaptable for literary
analysis.

ii

Emotive statements, of which ethical statements are one
sort (see Carnap below), are particularly subject to clouded,
illogical thought, because of the emotional nature of their
issues, which turns grammar to the service of affective considerations. Rudolf Carnap, in his essay "The Rejection of Metaphysics" makes this very clear:

> It is easy to see that it is merely a difference
> of formulation, whether we state a norm or a value
> judgment. A norm or rule has an imperative form,
> for instance: "do not kill!" The corresponding
> value judgment would be "Killing is evil." This
> difference of formulation has become practically
> very important, especially for the development of
> philosophical thinking. The, "Do not kill," has
> grammatically the imperative form and will there-
> fore not be regarded as an assertion. But the
> value statement, "Killing is evil," although, like
> the rule it is merely an expression of a certain
> wish, has the grammatical form of a declarative
> sentence.[3]

Carnap's point is so obvious as to be dazzling. The pene-
tration of his insight into grammatical equivalents is undis-
puted, as is its potential for havoc in philosophical and ordinary language users' circles. Certainly, questions of good
and evil have been taken "au grand sérieux" by philosophers
for centuries. And countless well-meaning individuals have
made life decisions on the same basis. And now to be told that

---

[3]Rudolf Carnap, Philosophy and Logical Syntax (London
1935), pp. 23-24.

their judgments are all attributable to grammatical misinterpretation!

Two issues emerge from Carnap's exposé. The first is the difference between using an expression and being able to say how we use it. The other is the conflict between psychological and logical thinking. The actual difference between <u>use</u> of language (where "use" implies what happens in practice), and functioning (the descriptive, retracing process), obviously furnishes much meat for analysis, especially where language is employed as suggestion or compulsion. This entails our second point, that the discrepancy between a statement's intention and a cool look at its actual logical unfolding, is or can be the realm of psychology. In Carnap's example, an emotion-laden issue is concealed behind the seeming difference of meaning of the two grammatical forms; psychological persuasion is the other side of the question. This persuasion is unveiled by close analysis of the language involved. While talking about psychology, at least classical psychology, we can't forget symbols and symbol-making. This is one of literature's outlets on the question of use and meaning.

iii

Logical thought resembles a good surgical operation--it is neat and painless. It proceeds from "p" to "not q" without worrying about the tone or mood with which these statements are uttered. It deals preferentially with formulations of the most general sort, genuine paradigms. "If all men are mortal and Socrates is a man, then Socrates is mortal," is not really about Socrates, as it seems. Any name would do. He is just one of those few unfortunates to get caught exemplifying a logical concept that transcends his actual death. His immortality is in fact guaranteed by his reproduction as the object of a

syllogism in hundreds of thousands of books about logic. The
advantage for logicians of general statements is that they are
widely applicable (at the extremes, they are tautologies).
And statements denuded of all sensual, concrete particulars
get the most mileage. (Witness the wide popularity enjoyed
by P and Q.)

But even positivists come down from the clouds occasionally to indulge in the palpitating examples furnished by a world
of matter. And this is the opportunity for humanists to raise
their eyes and point to the manifest violations of purity that
enter as soon as the realm of P and Q is left behind. Positivist philosophers themselves are not unconscious of the pollu-
tions of associational thinking. Its omnipresence has led some
of them[4] to set up two distinct categories, those of "factual
representations" and "object representations." The first would
be something simple, the existence of which is certain, like
saying "there is a chair," and being able to point to a chair
in the next room. An object representation, on the other hand,
would be to say "there is a chair," but to associate with it
the many pleasant afternoons spent reading in it. This additional association is not part of the statement, "there is a
chair" in any theoretically solid way, but it is nonetheless
an ineluctable part of the mental process, the conclusion of
which is, "there is a chair." As Carnap points out, even so
dry a topic as geometry is not immune to associational thinking, or "object representations." The presence of diagrams
is not an intrinsic part of classical geometry; they are as
superfluous as thinking wistfully of a favorite chair. But
since such diagrams are often used as a teaching aid, their
presence as "object representations" is of practical consequence.

---

[4]Notably Carnap

Literature is another beneficiary of associational thinking; this is, in fact, one of its prime methods for enlarging
the scope of its ontology. Such association is often unconscious, the product of long training in figurative habits of
thinking. In a way, a logician's despair is an artist's delight.
But there is no reason why literature, as a product of language,
should not be capable of undergoing scrutiny on the subject of
its object representations. If literature is a created product,
put together piece by piece, syllable by syllable, it deserves
more than false respect, ceremonial glimpses which remain at
surface level, courteously ignoring the underpinnings.

In speaking of associational thought, we are often, though
not always, speaking of metaphor. Metaphor is literature's
trump card, and it is difficult to avoid it even in speaking
about literature (at least in this essay). Logicians, however,
seem to have anticipated this problem by writing as literally
as possible, and, in some cases, relegating metaphor to the
status of a "category mistake." By this they mean that metaphorical language is misplaced associational language which un-
justifiably combines two or more different ontological categories and considers the combination logical. This concept obviously bears further inquiry in the examination of actual texts,
since it is seductively easy to make such assertions in abstraction, when not faced with perfect metaphors that seem startlingly
apt and logical.

iv

There is also another area of concern for the language
analysts which bears on the question of metaphor. This is the
difference that Frege points to between "Sinn" and "Bedeutung."
"Sinn," or sense, although that isn't the only translation,
and "Bedeutung," or denotation, are two poles of meaning in

language. The denotation of a word, is more or less what you
can point to, while the sense is the way or ways you approach
the word in describing it. This is something like the more
familiar distinction between denotation and connotation. The
example Frege gives of this difference is the two terms, "morning star" and "evening star," both of which mean Venus. The
two descriptions have the same denotation, "Venus," but different senses. There is also a third term which joins these
others, and that is "representation." So the three levels according to Frege would now be, the object that is denoted, a
representation of that object, and, in between the two, the
sense of the object, which is not as subjective as the representation, but not the object, either. Representations here
are completely subjective. Any number of people can understand
the sense of a word, but no two people can have an identical
representation of it. And on the subject of representations
Frege demonstrates a pronounced aesthetic consciousness:

> Zu den hier noch möglichen Unterschieden gehören
> die Färbungen und Beleuchtungen, welche Dichtkunst
> Beredsamkeit dem Sinne zu geben suchen. Diese
> Färbungen und Beleuchtungen sind nicht objectiv,
> sondern jeder Hörer und Leser muss sie sich selbst
> nach den Winken des Dichters oder Redners
> hinzuschaffen. Ohne eine Verwandtschaft des
> menschlichen Vorstellens wäre freilich die Kunst
> nicht möglich; wieweit aber den Absichten des
> Dichters entsprochen wird, kann nie genau ermittelt
> werden.[5]

This is a somewhat unusual demonstration of tolerance on
the part of a language analyst, particularly because the exact
relation between words and what they represent is usually
uppermost in their thought (even when they are denying any such

---

[5]Gottlob Frege, "Über Sinn und Bedeutung" _Zeitschrift
für Philosophie und philosophische Kritik_ 100 (1892), p. 31.

relation). But here, Frege seems to be speaking of a specific, internal representation. In order for humans to be able to communicate with one another at all, a vague resemblance between representations is necessary, but this need not, and really cannot, be an identical resemblance. This is where the creativity of interpretation enters, why a single poem can be analyzed innumerable times, without being used up in the process. Representations should differ; they are free to demonstrate their subjectivity. But the sense of a word should be understood by anyone hearing it.

Yet sense, too, may be a source of confusion and differing opinions. Returning to the same example, if a person doesn't happen to know that "Morning star" and "Evening star" refer to the same thing, he might find a synonymous use of them erroneous. Fortunately, the truth of a proposition doesn't reside in its sense, but in its denotation, in the object it ultimately points to. So confusion in sense wouldn't be very serious in any far-reaching terms, although it presents difficulties for the isolated, ill-informed individual. And ideally, in some perfect language, such a confusion would not be possible; sense and denotation would have a one-to-one relationship in that a particular description would always denote a single object. But such a univocity is at the moment neither desirable nor possible in a literary work.

We cited Frege's invitation to multiple interpretation above, in his discussion of representation. But the same freedom of multiple interpretation can exist in the sense/denotation distinction, particularly as applied to metaphor. Metaphor may be a category mistake, as was suggested earlier. But it may also be the normal fluctuation between the sense of a statement and its denotation. While the denotation stays the same, the sense of any statement may vary at will. In this way we not only ratify metaphor, but call upon it to demonstrate by its presence the actual working of a language, according to logical rules of meaning. Literature takes a tremulous step forward.

The denotation of a word or proposition is usually the most objective part of it. All roads lead to Rome, and all linguistic signs point to this denotation. It is only because of the stability of this denoted object that the sense of a word may vary as it does, without completely destroying conceptual schemes. But in actual use, there are times when the sense of a word is appropriate, but its denotation isn't. As Frege, to cover all contingencies, reminds us, "morning star" doesn't always, absolutely mean "Venus."

V

These kinds of concerns seem very fruitful for literature, because, while they present literature with certain rules, they also allow it to deploy itself in a rather rangy camp. Literature is not crammed here into an iron maiden of strictures governing literature's sensible manifestations. On the contrary, Frege's scheme treats literature like a spoiled child, pats it on the head, rationalizes its foibles, observes it closely to see whether it can adhere to the existing rules, and if not, creates other rules which seem to describe it better. The charge might be leveled here of Frege's bending the rules, something a logical positivist does not want to be found guilty of. But in the case where language is the object of these rules, such an unyielding attitude seems short-sighted. Because rules in this case are not normative, rather descriptive. After basic grammar, one doesn't legislate how people speak; one notes and describes. This is a most appropriate point of view for literature, whose purpose (if it has any) is to push language as far as it will go, forcing analysts to create new rules that encompass its freaks and capers.

Language often, in fact, transcends the objects it is said to be about. Even positivists like Bertrand Russell concede language's mermaid powers:

> Language, . . . though a useful and even indispensable tool, is a dangerous one, since it begins by suggesting a definiteness, discreteness, and quasi-permanence in objects which physics seems to show that they do not possess.[6]

So Gutenberg was more than an economic phenomenon. He was a modifier of the natural world, permitting words to arrange themselves in straight lines that hinted at monuments. What Russell is probably thinking about here is that naming a table is not really encompassing the billions of moving atoms that make up its structure. And saying "atom" isn't really talking about all the sub-particles that we've come to associate with this configuration, ad infinitum. A certain amount of short-hand is necessary so that each linguistic emission doesn't become a laborious process demanding hours. And anyway, would the false concreteness of language be an issue in literature? If, like Zola, we were concerned with presenting a hyper-realistic world picture, then the question might interest us, albeit not on the sub-atomic level. But, at a certain point, particularly in literature, one has to accept "language" as given, as found, with all its defects on its back. If language is giving a false impression of permanence, then that _is_ language, that is the object we're dealing with. Our microstructural concerns might then shift to language's own composition, to its logical syntax as the fixer of its structure and possibilities, to the compulsions of style.

---

[6]Bertrand Russell, Human Knowledge: Its Scope and Limits (New York 1948), p. 76.

vi

There seem to be two views of language at work here. One
is the magisterial view--language as furnisher of permanence
and ontological consequence, shaping mere events to its imperious
will, making "things" significant in an Adamic naming-riot.
The other view is language itself hemmed-in by the constraints
of its structure, being able to approach the real world only
after careful syntactic analysis of its actual capabilities.

Since different languages have different syntactical ar-
rangements, these formal constraints are partially a social matter. And, having admitted this (if, in fact, we have) it is difficult these years to resist the temptation to regard language
as a dialectical phenomenon--as the tool which society has created to tyrannize over society, to limit finally its possibilities for expression. We see the axe falling daily, with television talk, for example, whose vocabulary and creative formulations shrink in proportion to the enlarging base of the pyra-
mid which is its audience. Television time is precious, so there
is always a market for neologisms and spongy phrases which "say
it all" in under thirty seconds. Concepts get compacted and
simplified; rhyme takes the place of sense, and the imitative
faculties of the audience are exploited unmercifully. Such a
trend obviously doesn't lead to the grand style, or to largeness
and boldness of thought. It does lead to efficiency, comfortable uniformity of utterance, and consequent suspicion of language
which "breaks the mold" (to borrow an expression from some
slightly-dated technology).

But this is the dark side of language, the one always cited
by dyspeptic Marxists whose television sets have just broken.
Whether language is a shrinking product of postindustrial civi-
lization, or the tyrant of all created things, is largely a

matter of indifference to the language analysts. Russell himself, after briefly throwing up his hands in the face of language's possibilities for reordering the world, has elsewhere[7]
proceeded, in shirtsleeves and with knife and fork, to create
a theory of descriptions which qualifies even the occurrence
of proper names, once a sacrosanct province, as Homer's and the
Bible's genealogies demonstrate. The glorious autonomy of such
a listing, carried along by its own rhythm and sense of purpose,
is drily challenged by logicians' considering even some proper
names as descriptions, rather than de facto names. And descriptions can be challenged as to accuracy, while genuine, proper
names cannot; they are symbols. The distinction between description and names seems very tenuous, very open to interpretation,
but using the one as the other often results in logical errors,
which Russell demonstrates in this now classic essay, considered
a model of paradigmatic thought. We'll look more closely at
the essay in a later chapter.

vii

Given the difficulty of using descriptions correctly, and
even of naming, it is hard to agree with Wittgenstein in the
Tractatus, that language can be a picture of the world. The
elements in a picture are presumably finite and definite, even
though a discussion of that same picture might be inexhaustible.
On the simplest level, therefore, a picture displaying its form
is quantitatively different from the language in which such a
form would be couched. And if we are treating reality as something that can be pictured, it would seem that we are faced with
a similar problem. To put it more exactly, we are creating a

---

[7]In his chapter called "Descriptions," from Introduction
to Mathematical Philosophy (London 1919).

picture, a mimesis of reality, by using language to display that picture. This involves a number of assumptions, both about reality and the language that is picturing it. First and most obvious, is reality such that it is completely describable or representable in language? The term "reality" in itself, is so nebulous and so productive of metaphysical debates, that to get behind that word to the mass of phenomena comprising it, is already an impressive achievement. And then, if language is to imitate reality, what does reality look like? What, for that matter, does language look like? Are we speaking here of the actual orthography, or the formation of individual letters? If that is our basis for reality, then reality must look very different in Arab countries. Maybe we should jump to syntax. There is some hope for that; according to our mood, the emphasis we want to give a sentence might vary considerably, and the syntax would often reflect this changed emphasis. But maybe this approach is too impressionistic, and anyway, are we really picturing our mood, or merely permitting the expression of it, which seems a little different.

But maybe we are being too literal. If language isn't a picture of reality (using "picture" now in the widest sense) what is it a picture of? Is it not itself part of reality, with its feet in it, so to speak? Can we speak or think in any way that gets us away from reality completely? Isn't even nonsense governed by the exact extent to which it departs from a sense of the real? If language is not a picture of reality, then it is not an opposing picture of anything else, either. It arises from real states of mind, it emerges from real vocal chords, and it enters ears which evaluate these sound waves and turn the fragments into meaningful patterns. We thus take refuge in a strictly empirical position, not a little ashamed at this summary retreat. But the question has been, and will be debated so much, that language becomes, not a picture of reality, but a wearied monument to discussions of language as such a picture. And we've done our bit to fill in a hollow of elbow, or to dab at a chin.

viii

We've been discussing a rather radical and unsubtle question--is language a picture of reality. It seems on reflection a little too large for comfortable discussion. Or maybe it's too large for uncomfortable discussion, since comfortable discussion of over-sized issues is supremely easy, but leads to the bad habit of pointing at things. A different but related question is that involving the issues of subjectivity and communication, or, more explicitly, are we able to communicate private, subjective states so that they would be intelligible to others while still being true to the states described. This is still part of the question, is language a picture of reality, but the reality is an internal, private one, and the language of the sort which can possibly make that internal reality a visible picture to all comers.

The prototype of an approach to this question is furnished by Wittgenstein in sections 243-317 of his Philosophical Investigations.[8] This is an extremely sensitive, extremely unanalyzable fragment of the Investigations that talks about pain and how one person's pain could be communicated to others. In spite of being philosophy, or "doing philosophy," as Wittgenstein always puts it, the fragment is almost in the form of a dramatic monologue (or dialogue with an implicit person who launches imagined objections). His distinctions are as finely cut as,

---

[8]Ludwig Wittgenstein, Philosophical Investigations (Oxford 1953), p. 88e-104e.

"Other people cannot be said to learn of my sensations only
from my behaviour,--for I cannot be said to learn of them. I
have them." His imagination is as wide-ranging as, "Are we perhaps over-hasty in our assumption that the smile of an unweaned
infant is not a pretence?--And on what experience is our assumption based? (Lying is a language game that needs to be learned
like any other one)."

From these two small pieces (and there are numerous others,
all equally striking), it is evident that Wittgenstein's "doing
philosophy" differs radically from that of other philosophers.
Wittgenstein is at once theoretical, organized, deeply reflec-
tive, and completely irresponsible. His analytic discursis of
what the sensation of pain really means to the sufferer is constantly interrupted by Confucian-like remarks such as, "Here
I should like to say: a wheel that can be turned though nothing
else moves with it, is not part of the mechanism." His method
is almost Socratic, and seems to imply that only an indirect
grasp of what he says is possible or even desirable. Mostly,
he is a man who writes for himself and clearly enjoys it, feeling no responsibility to drag the uncomprehending multitude along
by the nose. His examples, however, are not of arcane nature;
practically all of them come from the realm of the sensuous, in
which he revels with minute interest: "Nor do you think that
really you ought to point to the colour with your hand, but with
your attention. (Consider what it means "to point to something
with the attention".)

In this fragment, Wittgenstein is almost indulging in
phenomenology, or epistemology, most unlike the other language
analysts, and especially unlike his method in his earlier work,
the Tractatus, which is much "drier," much more concerned with
impersonal phenomena like "states of affairs" (Sachverhalten).
But in spite of the more sensuous nature of this section, the

sensuality is accompanied by a strong refusal to be pinned down.
Even though we seem to be taking refuge in the body as a source
of examples of a private, bodily language, any conclusive move
in this direction is deftly eschewed by Wittgenstein. A part
of the body feels pain, but it is very hard to say precisely how
this pain is displayed, or how we <u>know</u> that part of the body is
in pain. As Wittgenstein reminds us, if we know someone has a
pain in his hand, we feel pity for that person; we look into
the sufferer's face, the expression of which is obviously not
directly connected with a pain in the hand. And, even if we
know we have a particular pain, there seems for Wittgenstein
finally no way that we can both express this pain so it's clear
to us, and tell others about it, so they will know exactly what
we are feeling. Our private, emotive language can never be communicable, since it lacks the laws of ordinary discourse by
which such discourse is rendered intelligible. It is as
Wittgenstein says, as though every person had a box with something that was called a "beetle" in it, but no one could look
into another person's box, so no one would know what another
person would consider a beetle. More dismal yet, the object in
the box might conceivably change, or even disappear, without the
knowledge of anyone else. The picture for Wittgenstein is really
a dark one, concerning the possibilities for communication of
private, subjective emotion to other existents. Language that
was truly subjective would have to be considered unformulable;
if you could state something in intelligible terms, then it would,
conversely, not really be subjective.

Somewhat as a commentary on what you can formulate and what
you can't, at most an aside--there are a lot of italicized words
in this piece of writing. There seems to be a real division
between what you can formulate in writing and what you can say,
the implication being that the emphasis given to language while

speaking it appreciably changes its meaning. Italicizing a word
is a way of vocalizing it, writing's equivalent of an oral, tonal
differentiation. So the question of our aside is, if there is
a difference between private, subjective language and language
that serves as communication is there also a difference between
writing language and speaking it? Would the Wittgenstein essay
say the same thing(s) if italics were not used?

It is difficult to say. Each sentence, obviously, would
be structurally the same, i.e., the syntax wouldn't change in
any way. But the possibilities for isolation of words or concepts so as to differentiate them from adjoining or similar words
would be greatly reduced. The difference between "*my* pain and
his pain," for example, would not be as clear-cut. Without italics, in fact, the phrase "my pain and his pain" might be taken
to mean a *shared* pain, just the *opposite* of what Wittgenstein
intended. (It's obvious that italics are becoming indispensable
to me, too, in this discussion of the use of italics.) When
Wittgenstein talks about *this* pain, or *meaning* instead of meaning, he is really speaking a new, encoded language, encoded because familiar words are being used but their ontology has
shifted. Each of these italicized words, in addition to their
original signification, contains an implicit addendum (*this* pain--
not the other one; *meaning*--not just referring to, etc.). But
inasmuch as the addendum is not clearly stated, can really only
be approximated, it becomes Wittgenstein's own form of private
language. Addenda like this are epistemological vacuums, the
area of words spoken to oneself, hinted at but not revealed to
the listener (reader).

Not only is this italicized language an expression of
Wittgenstein's own sentiments, but it is also a way of talking
about a private language. Sections 243-317 of the *Investigations*
demonstrate in general the impossibility of describing a private,

subjective language. They do this by making very sensitive, minute statements about pain behavior and other perceptive phenomena (is my sense of red the same as another person's?). And in spite of the utmost delicacy and discernment of this slow dissection, Wittgenstein concludes that truly private language is not communicable. But I am maintaining that Wittgenstein has communicated a form of private language in his use of italics. He has made overt public statements whose meaning has in large measure been vitiated or at least modified by the italics they contain. Vast areas of private, illicit language use are suggested by these sack-like expressions. Of course, the difficulty in all of this would be a demand for the exact equivalents to these italicized words, and this obviously, cannot be furnished. So Wittgenstein maintains a sort of autonomy over his own private language, and the kinds of private language suggested in this fragment. But a slight encroachment is possible, a confinement of this private language to an even narrower space, if one calls into question this immersion in italics. It is perhaps a tiny area where language use leaps ahead of language-consciousness, even in so hyper-conscious a person as Wittgenstein.

ix

We have (quite illicitly) been applying a sort of literary analysis to a series of philosophical statements, to see what a kind of literary language-consciousness can tell us about the world. In effect, while philosophy was pursuing its object, literary analysis in the sense of close attention to style, was pursuing the pursuer, not for any other reason than to play with the question of private language, since Wittgenstein is undoubtedly one of the most inscrutable philosophers. He himself plays constantly, and felicitously, even while maintaining an ever-present rigor in his use of concepts.

Can these concepts be of use to literature? How does the idea of a private language apply to literature? On one level, there will always be a discrepancy between what an author writes and what we read. This shadowy area would be for the language analysts pure metaphysics, the realm of conceptual rules that don't quite mesh. And there is in fact, a neat tautology shared by many of these philosophers that if something is a concept, it <u>has</u> to be clear, because clarity is part of the definition of a concept. Nevertheless, there seems to be a real practical problem in sorting out an author's intentions or original set of ideas, and that which filters through to the audience (as well as in the audience's response, which occasionally makes it way back to the author: "But I wasn't writing a satire!") The private language of author and audience consists in the fact that each has a sort of affective repertoire which he parades for the respective purpose of reading or writing. Often these repertoires are very similar in the two cases, since author and audience have presumably inherited certain shared cultural attitudes which brought them together in the first place. But the symbiosis of literature and criticism we spoke of earlier seems fatal to mutual comprehension. The author, in writing for his critics (and they are everywhere, don't be fooled), and the critics, putting themselves in the author's place, seem somehow able to brush past each other without feeling a thing. Private language on both sides, instead of diminishing in this way, seems to thicken, in this double anticipation of motives.

There is also another possible form of private language, that which occurs between author and created characters. An author may well create a set of characters and then lose control of them. He may sketch in some outlines and a number of

speeches, and then see this language go far beyond what he intended, perhaps in response to certain subconscious associations
or unspoken critical paranoias. The characters' speech may indeed be a private language, the language of imaginary creations,
which can't be the same as that of their living counterparts.
Because the speech of the living must reconcile thought and lan-
guage--their language is deepened by the obstacle that thought
creates, the tussle between what one wants to say and what one
can actually, finally say. This kind of conflict is totally
lacking to literary characters. Their speech is assigned, one
dimensional. They are totally what they say, since speech for
them is almost their entire ontology. Pirandello has shown this
very aptly in his Sei personaggi, has, in fact, almost exhausted
the subject, which works far better in a play than in an essay.
Without the thickening resonance conferred by a flesh and blood
existence, language is tinny, self-consciously present. It is
private language in the sense of being deceptive; at best, it
resembles human speech, all is there in the words, and for precisely that reason, only about half the meaning is there.

A last example of private language in literature would be
the one furthest from Wittgenstein's imagination--where one character speaks a language which cannot be understood by another
character in the same work. Can one character have any truly
private emotions which he cannot communicate to another character in accordance with logical rules of discourse? A different
way of saying this would be, is there some area of a character's
existence that we can sketch out but not pin down, because it
remains confined to some internal scheme which neither we nor
another character can fathom? We said earlier that the language
of literary characters must be different from that of human beings. And of course this is true. But if the language of these
characters apes that of the world, then do the same linguistic,

analytic rules apply? And if they do, would there be the same area of non-adherence to rules, i.e., private language? These are questions which might not be answerable at this stage of our work, without texts to look at. And they might not be answerable at all, because they may be nonsense.

Beckett apparently took this and similar questions seriously enough. In both plays and novels, he parades a set of characters whose language is often unintelligible to one another. The characters make speeches in what seems to be an ordinary declamatory style, but not even close examination reveals that what they are saying is not making sense in the usual way. I qualify "not making sense," because the form of the speeches suggests that they may make sense in some other context, or ontology. They are a seeming private language which is peculiar to the character who is speaking. Of course we know that Beckett's now somewhat dated message is the Sartrian total isolation of each of us with respect to others or to a god who in some way unifies creation. Speaking nonsense, being unable to communicate sense, is one symptom of the problem. And so is speaking in a style designed to thwart inquiry. Or uttering a linguistic cry of pain or desire.

x

Related to private language, but not quite identical to it, is the question of imaging and imagination raised by Gilbert Ryle in his book, The Concept of Mind. Following a long tradition of attempts at cognitive description, heralded by such people as Coleridge and Hume, Ryle wants to know exactly what people are doing when they are imaging or using their imagination. These terms encompass a very wide range of activities, or quasi-activities, but in general they are all mental or pseudo-activities. We shouldn't hasten to use the word "activities"

because Ryle even questions the fact of their being activities
at all. His entire argument is so subtle and yet so sustained,
that it is difficult to do him much justice by paraphrasing.
It is probably better to present a few passages, so we can begin
to locate the areas of Ryle's concerns. We will be dealing primarily with the chapter of the book entitled "Imagination," which
is where Ryle most clearly sets forth his ideas on the subject.

Ryle begins by furnishing a very general statement of his
purpose:

> I attempt in this chapter to show that to try to
> answer the question, 'Where do the things and hap-
> penings exist which people imagine existing?' is
> to try to answer a spurious question. They do not
> exist anywhere, though they are imagined as existing,
> say, in this room, or in Juan Fernandez.
> The critical problem is that of describing what
> is 'seen in the mind's eye' and what is 'heard in
> one's head'. What are spoken of as 'visual images',
> 'mental pictures', 'auditory images' and, in one
> use, 'ideas' are commonly taken to be entities
> which are genuinely found existing and found existing
> elsewhere than in the external world. So minds are
> nominated for their theatres.[9]

This then, in general terms is the preconception that Ryle
will seek to destroy or alter. And it might be considered a
rather arduous undertaking. Because no one can deny the familiar sound these locutions have for us. Almost everybody (probably including Ryle in one of his giddy moments) has been guilty
at one time or another (most more frequently than that) of using
such a formula and feeling it to be an adequate description of
his state of mind at the time. One can hardly blame a language
user of this sort. There is nothing on the surface of language
to make this usage sound grotesque. It on the contrary sounds

---

[9]Gilbert Ryle, The Concept of Mind (London 1949) p. 245.

and feels like the correct explanation of what is happening
to us, the sensibility behind the face. But as Ryle hastens
to disconcert us, "much as stage-murders do not have victims and
are not murders, so seeing things in one's mind's eye does not
involve either the existence of things seen or the occurrence
of acts of seeing them. So no asylum is required for them to
exist or occur in" (p. 245). This analogy, however far we are
at this point from feeling it to be correct, begins to show
the complexity and multiplicity of Ryle's thought. He quite
effortlessly leaps from presumptive mental activity to the action on a stage, encircling them both with language that finds
equivalents. And in the rest of the chapter, Ryle will, in
fact, deal with activities of an imagined nature, and those of
a mock or pretended nature. His genius resides in his showing
us the similarities of the two.

As Ryle is a language analyst, he is never far from attri-
buting to misuse of language the errors we make in perception.
Thus, in speaking of imagination, he says:

> As visual observation has preeminence over obser-
> vation by the other senses, so with most people
> visual imagination is stronger than auditory,
> tactual, . . . imagination, and consequently the
> language in which we discuss these matters is
> largely drawn from the language of seeing. Peo-
> ple speak, for example, of 'picturing' or 'vis-
> ualizing' things, but they have no corresponding
> generic verbs for imagery of the other sorts . . .
> I want to show that the concept of picturing,
> visualizing or 'seeing' is a proper and useful
> concept, but that its use does not entail the
> existence of pictures which we contemplate or the
> existence of a gallery in which such pictures
> are ephemerally suspended. Roughly, imaging oc-
> curs but images are not seen (p. 247).

These lines present us with the broad picture (you'll
pardon the expression) of Ryle's main argument. The language

of seeing, which we justifiably apply to the physical action
of seeing external objects, is in large measure responsible for
the errors we make in talking about 'seeing' in the imagination.
Ryle carefully distinguishes between physical seeing and this
other kind of 'seeing.' The quotation marks indicate that in
the latter activity, we are not really seeing anything. Ryle
completes this part of the discussion with an example that only
years of attention to language use could have made possible:

> True, a person picturing his nursery is, in a cer-
> tain way, like that person seeing his nursery,
> but the similarity does not consist in his really
> looking at a real likeness of his nursery, but in
> his really seeming to see his nursery itself,
> when he is not really seeing it. He is not be-
> ing a spectator of a resemblance of his nursery,
> but he is resembling a spectator of his nursery
> (p. 248).

It is desirable to read this passage at least two or three
times in order to exhaust its ramifications. We leave that
task to the reader, only hoping he will not go the length of taking a long and expensive trip to the scenes of his early bliss,
in order to test the theory. But a very short paraphrase of
the passage would be that a person imagining his nursery would
not be seeing any object, but would be playing the part of seeing an object.

Again, this passage suggests the relationship between
imagining and the act of pretending. Ryle devotes an entire
section of the chapter to pretending, under which heading he
subsumes such diverse activities as "cheating, acting a part,
playing bears, shamming sick and hypochondria" (p. 258). So
for Ryle, "pretending" is obviously a broader term than it sounds
to us. And he does, in fact, describe it very ingeniously:

> To describe someone as pretending is to say that
> he is playing a part, and to play a part is to

> play the part, normally, of someone who is not
> playing a part, but doing or being something in-
> genuously or naturally . . . . Pretending to growl
> like a bear, or lie still like a corpse, is a
> sophisticated performance, where the bear's growl-
> ing and the corpse's immobility are naive. (p.
> 259)

The truth of this relation between pretending and being is so
obvious that it doesn't always occur to us. 'Playing the part
of someone who is not playing a part' is certainly a dive into
the limits of ontology, while remaining an accurate and even
simple observation.

Elsewhere, Ryle exemplifies this form of intentionality
by describing the activities of a forger. He, too, is intent
upon playing a part well:

> But forging a signature is quite unlike signing;
> the one requires what the other does not, the wish
> and ability to produce marks indistinguishable from
> a signature . . . Deliberate verisimilitude is a
> part of the concept of copying. The very like-
> nesses between copies and their originals are what
> make activities of copying different in type from
> the activities copied. (p. 260)

As Ryle pointed out earlier in the chapter, the sense of
the perfection or imperfection of a copy or imitation is reflected
in the language we use to talk about these imitations, just as
the vocabulary of physical seeing furnishes the verbs for mental or imaginative activities. Thus, Ryle reminds us, we will
readily talk about a doll as lifelike or not lifelike, but we
don't talk about a baby in those terms. The same is true for
whether or not an actor is "convincing," but not whether a person is convincing. Whenever we are testifying to the similarity
or accuracy of something in this sense, we can't be talking about
an original.

There is one more point we should mention in connection
with Ryle's theory of imaging. That is the foreknowledge and

restraint that are required in the exercise of imaging. In other
words, you have to know how to do what you are imagining, or how
what you are imagining goes, and yet refrain from doing it. As
Ryle illustrates:

> We might say that imagining oneself talking or
> humming is a series of abstentions from producing
> the noises which would be the due words or notes
> to produce, if one were talking or humming aloud.
> That is why such operations are impenetrably se-
> cret; not that the words or notes are being pro-
> duced in a hermetic cell, but that the operations
> consist of abstentions from producing them . . .
> Refraining from saying things, of course, entails
> knowing both what one would have said and how one
> would have said it. (pp. 269-70)

There seems to be a balance here between ability and pre-
paredness, and the sort of negative energy which subverts and
keeps these qualities under cover. It is again, another way
of looking at the difference between being a corpse and playing a corpse. The former state requires no special ability or
observation of the laws of nature. It occurs naturally, and
its genuineness cannot be doubted. The latter, however, involves
knowing exactly what a corpse is, how it looks and acts. Playing a corpse means, among other things, abstaining from being
naturally and unconsciously dead. Lack of consciousness would
seriously impair one's ability to imitate.

I am undoubtedly straining the example past the point of
rigor mortis. The main idea to be grasped here, at least for
our purposes, is the way imaging as a form of behavior verges
on Wittgenstein's idea of private language. It would be aw-
fully hard for one person to witness a series of abstentions in
another person. Yet that, according to Ryle, would be the way
to describe almost all imaginative activities. We can carry
this one step further and question the fact of Ryle's knowing

how to describe imaginative processes which are, according to
him, impenetrably secret.

But this is just one example of a whole series of problems
which are all of the same type--how do we talk about language
without using language? How do we move the world, without
having another place to stand? The answer is, we don't. We
use language, since we must; we move the world by internal
activations. There is no question but that the means are faulty,
"unscientific," and even possibly, doomed to failure. But it
is also true that we have no choice. Analysts of language,
nuclear physicists, tread a narrow path of their own choosing,
a path that would be much easier to walk if they lacked brain
cells and vocal chords, if they didn't occupy space in the physical world. But failing to satisfy these criteria, they nevertheless remain stubbornly on that path, defending to the death
their right to an illogical position.

We, too, want to walk that path, along the sheltered ar-
cade hollowed out by the illogical language analysts. We want
their ontological death to contribute to our life, and to the
life of literature, our sworn object. The following chapters
will use the hard-won logico-linguistic considerations of these
philosophers, as set forth in this chapter, and as they arise
in discussion, with the hope that they will be a fresher way
of looking at literature, or at least, will contribute something
to the already large panoply of critical tools. The path yawns.

C H A P T E R   I I

THE RAPE OF THE RAPE OF THE LOCK

i

In Chapter I we did a lot of parading. The resemblance
of literary criticism to literature flashed past, followed by
the more sober tread of the language analysts, whose view of
literature is, if not quite hostile, then not completely trust-
ing, either. We arrayed some of the concerns of these analysts,
a spectrum ranging from demands for verifiability to the advantages of non-factual representations, which we have been calling associational thinking. And we found small ways in which
these concerns might ultimately be of interest or use to literature, at least in general.

But now instead of parading, we might do some trudging.
We have somehow to get from the stratum of ideas to that of
textual details. We want to take some of the thoughts of these
philosophers and force ourselves to look at literature (in this
case Pope's Rape of the Lock) through this special lens. The
strain will be severe. Because there seems to be a considerable disjunction between the realm of concepts and that of their
application in analysis. This is surprising on reflection,
since it can be argued that concepts are intimately related to
particulars. But in spite of the fondest hopes of the language
analysts, who could probably imagine a concept made of trans-
parent plastic, into which one could look and see its constituents, there is a real struggle in fitting barren concepts into
their sensuous details. Particularly in so fallen a medium as
literature.

ii

One of the classic distinctions made by commentators on
language is the difference in style between the language of
science and that of a lyric poem. The difference in style is
obviously the result of a difference of intention--to state
something as clearly as possible in the one case, and as artis-
tically as possible in the other. And art and clarity are not
always synonymous. Neither, of course are scientific language
and clarity.

If scientific writing is unclear, how or why is it so?
Is it unclear to the extent that it has a style which might
be called literary? Or are we dealing with the same problem
of translating concepts into language? In other words, is it
language itself, with its bizarreries and conscious inexacti-
tudes, that is the culprit? Even in writing that seeks to be
as flat as possible? The answer is probably yes, and given
this, how much greater a potential for unclarity has literature,
in exploiting unclarities (calling them ambiguities). But literature somehow does not run the same risks as scientific writing,
since it confides itself confidently to language's care, instead
of fighting against it. More or less as one is told to fall.
In pushing language up front, into the world of sense, literature has freed itself from the contingency of struggling against
language. Unlike scientific writing, literature invites multiple interpretations. These interpretations are a major source
of difficulty for the application of principles of language
analysis. To play strictly by their rules, you have to be in
the state of attempting to say one thing, and then look at the
ways you've said more than one thing (or something different
from the one thing you intended). No! Stop! Wrong! Go back!
How can you dream of applying these concepts to literature?
You can't even write about them, except in a colloquial style!

Acknowledging these objections, what can we do about them?
How could it have occurred to us that these two areas of human
cerebration could ever meet? The simple, undisputably tauto-
logical answer is, language is language. Aside from very basic
and denuded languages, like those of mathematics or logic, there
doesn't seem to be any corner of linguistic symbolism that is
peculiar to a specific area of thought. Structuralists could
probably tell you with great exactitude which words or sorts
of words are more common to particular areas of concern, using
computers and great cataloguing zeal. But there is no way to
legislate absolutely the occurrence or nonoccurrence of individual words, however unlikely it is that these words would appear on a particular language-user's palate (next to his corned
beef). Since the stratum of ideas balances precariously on that
of language, we have no choice but to say that shared language
carries with it the potential for shared ideas, a kind of 'each
man's death diminishes me' of lexicography. All of this points
to the fact that language analysis should be capable of general
applicability, if it is to be valid for even one area.

So we come back to our original problem: Why not look
at Pope through the lenses furnished by these language analysts?
Why not make literature just a special case of language, rather
than hollowing out for literature a particular niche where it
can only be handled with the equivalent of New Criticism gloves.
What can this analysis tell us? In telling us what's being
said, it can also tell us what's not being said, the too-
often ignored literal meaning which promises the absent by
its presence. Analysis can also perhaps tell us what there
is about literature that is truly special, ways that language
is being used that on close observation prove unorthodox,
more (or less) than information-giving. And if information-
giving, then what sort of information? How many pounds in a

kilogram? How many tears on the pillow of a great queen? Or maybe what the English thought of lapdogs.

These concerns reflect very different spheres of experience, but their common ground is that all the answers exist potentially in the realm of language. The questions literature answers are all in this realm too. As are the things we want to say about literature. About The Rape of the Lock we can say various things, depending on the emphasis we want to give it. We can say, for example, that the poem is based on an actual incident. We can say too, that although based on this incident, the poem was written in an attempt to conciliate wounded feelings. A third thing is that the poem is written in an epic style. The fourth qualifies the third, and points out that it is a mock-epic, etc.

These are all true statements about the poem, but they are true in different ways. The first two tie the poem to real events, which literary history can bear out. But the first is a less slanted statement than the second, because the first involves the "simple" resemblance between what happened and what was recounted. The second, although a true statement, becomes more complicated, because we've entered the realm of emotive statements. In this sense the poem has a purpose other than that of telling an incident; it wants to influence feelings in the telling, so it could very well make use of the repertoire of persuasion, including such distortions of the truth as exaggerations, etc.

The third and fourth statements deal with a different conception of "true," truth that is true by convention. That we are ascribing to the poem an epic style means that in some way it resembles other writing that we have chosen to call epic. (It is obviously not metrically identical with our chosen epic prototype, the Iliad. But there are many sections of the Pope that resemble nothing so much as <u>Iliad</u> set pieces, or tropes, in that way justifying our calling it, "in the epic style.") The parenthesis concatenates the fourth statement. That we call the Pope a mock-epic involves the distance it has come from a real epic. The style is not identical, the subject is not "lofty," two sure signs of a "mock-epic." The language entailed in a mock-epic is a mixture of different and similar (with respect to a real epic). It can't be totally one or the other, because then there wouldn't be any room for "similarity in difference."[10] Without any similarity, we wouldn't be able to gauge difference, and vice-versa. Our definitions, which are themselves based on differences, would become distorted. An entire area of <u>a priori</u> truths would drop into endless night.

Lest this should happen, we have to look, not only at the words used, but at the way they are used. We mentioned earlier Carnap's example that "killing is evil" really means "Do not kill," even though the two sentences are very different in grammatical form and seem to be saying different things. The poetry of Pope can also be examined to determine what is really being said, how the language of the epic becomes mock-epic, and whether or not an altered use of language carries with it a psychological change of impact, as in Carnap's example.

iii

The <u>Rape of the Lock</u> is a very tight, crackling poem, almost any line of which is doing some significant job. So it is very hard to know just where to plunge in. To be arbitrary, let's look at lines 101-110 of Canto II:

---

[10]The Hegelian precept so abhorred by Bertrand Russell

> This Day, black Omens threat the
>   brightest Fair
> That e'er deserved a watchful
>   Spirit's Care;
> Some dire Disaster, or by Force,
>   or Slight,
> But what, or where, the Fates
>   have wrapt in Night.
> Whether the Nymph shall break
>   Diana's Law,
> Or some frail China Jar receive
>   a Flaw,
> Or stain her Honour, or her new
>   Brocade,
> Forget her Pray'rs, or miss a
>   Masquerade,
> Or lose her Heart, or Necklace,
>   at a Ball;
> Or whether Heav'n has doomed that
>   Shock must fall.[11]

What can we say about these lines? For one thing, that
there seems to be a split between the first four lines and the
last six. The first four lines tell us about some possible im-
pending doom, and the last six speculate as to what it might
be. Before the speculation begins, the announcement of doom
is very general, very unspecified. Words like 'omens,' 'disaster,' 'force,' 'Fates' come straight from the language of
epic, in general, but aside from that, do not particularize.
For the language analysts, such words would be largely non-referential, because as they stand they are just big formulations,
like the word "virtue," not able to point to anything concrete.
(There is a difference between saying, "Here is Virtue," and
"This man has X characteristics, which make us call him
virtuous.") So these first four lines seem to function as space-
holders, not really saying anything.

---

[11] Alexander Pope, Poetry and Prose, ed. Aubrey Williams,
(Boston 1969) p. 86. (All future Pope citations from the same
source.)

Literary (as opposed to language) analysts looking at these first four lines would say something different about them. They would say that these lines are in the epic style, because tropes like 'what or where the Fates have wrapt in Night' remind us strongly of Homer. And whether the lines made any sense or not, literary analysts would be correct in saying this. Combining these two points of view, one could say that these lines of Pope have a meaning to the precise extent that they are concretely meaningless. What are we saying? We are saying that the very emptiness and non-referential quality of these lines is what qualifies them as formulae, and it is because they are formulae that we know Pope is writing in an epic style. If the lines were more concrete they wouldn't be the epic style, they would be Pope's style, or Homer's style, or Milton's style, all of which are not identical with epic style. Style here is dependent on abstraction, and ultimately, on meaninglessness (from the Positivists' point of view).

We are viewing style in this case, not as something distinctive, but more as a unifying principle, like syntax. Pushing it even further, we could say style is the syntax of poetry. Style is an area most language analysts don't even deal with, even when rephrasing statements to make them more accurate. The resultant rephrasings are often clumsy and infelicitous, if more exact, and from this perspective, style is nothing more than embroidery. But there is a genuine logic to style, which governs the choice of one word over another, and ultimately influences sense. (Some might say style takes the place of sense, which is certainly possible.)

The last six lines quoted above are "Pope-style." They are, as we have said, in the epic tradition, but personalized. In enumerating the possible misfortunes the Fates have in mind,

Pope is telling in condensed form the general concerns of the poem. It is a neat and economical device, showing us what is important by naming what is threatened. Pope's style is often also a latinate juxtaposing of opposites--aut . . . aut in this case. Heroic couplets encourage the organic presentation of contrary ideas, because the metrical and rhyming similarity suggests an 'equal-but-different' status for these ideas. A dualistic worldview might be extrapolated from this, but we are getting far afield.

Although Pope is accomplishing a justifiable literary achievement, language analysts would say it is at the expense of logic. The following three lines would come in for the harshest censure: "Or stain her Honour, or her new Brocade, / Forget her Pray'rs, or miss a Masquerade, / Or lose her Heart, or Necklace, at a Ball." What's wrong with all these lines from a logical point of view is, in a word, they are all category mistakes. The often-quoted model for a category mistake is the sentence, "The lady came home in tears and in a sedan chair." A longer but perhaps more comprehensible example of a category mistake is the one Gilbert Ryle gives in his The Concept of Mind:

> A foreigner visiting Oxford or Cambridge for the first time is shown a number of colleges, libraries, playing fields, museums, scientific departments, and administrative offices. He then asks, 'But where is the University? . . .' It has then to be explained to him that the University is not another collateral institution, some ulterior counterpart to the colleges, laboratories and offices which he has seen. The University is just the way in which all that he has already seen is organized.[12]

This example, and that of the lady in the sedan chair, are quite different, but they both deal with ways in which

---

[12]Ryle, op. cit., p. 16

language is incorrectly used. With the Oxford example, the
concept of "University" doesn't mean the same thing as that
of "library." "University" is in itself an empty concept, only
fleshed out by its concrete parts. It is their sum, and method
of organization, but it is not equivalent to them.

The description of the lady in the sedan chair is also
a false equating of two non-parallel language uses, yoked together by seeming similarity of form. In this case the incorrect usage is readily apparent to English speakers, and its
effect is comic. The Oxford example involves a more complex
misunderstanding that could lead to difficulties on the campus.
The common element to both is a confusion about the functioning of language.

In the lines of Pope cited above, we also have a form
of category mistake. The line, "Or stain her Honour, or her
new Brocade," is certainly implying a parallelism in its shared
use of the verb, "stain." The two nouns, "Honour," and "Bro -
cade," both depend on this verb. But they are obviously very
different sorts of words. 'Honour,' in logical positive terms,
is a meaningless word, which doesn't point to anything. In
grammatical terms, it has some substance as an "abstract noun,"
but this is only to hold a place for it in a grammar which seeks
to explain everything, and enumerate what it cannot explain.
In terms of something representable, "honour" has no meaning.

Brocade, on the other hand, is rather specific, referring
as it does to a type of dress material, or in this case, to
the dress itself. To stain honor is certainly a possible expression in English. And daily, anguished testimony presents us
with the possibility of staining a fabric. But the parallelism of the two could hardly be maintained in experiential terms.
Nor is it usually attempted. But chez Pope, the barest edge
of the possible becomes the actual; the sin is committed; the
illogical juxtaposition is effected.

Is the category mistake here just like the others? In a sense it isn't, because both instances of "stain" with its respective objects are bona fide English usages (unlike the equivalence of "University" and "library"). But a category mistake still exists in the assignment of the same value to 'Honour' and 'Brocade.' We have shown that they are not compatible in concreteness, but they are also not compatible in emotive connotation. Few representations of "brocade" would be identical; every other person would probably imagine a slightly different fabric when the word was mentioned. This is very much in keeping with the liberty granted to representations by Frege, which we pointed to earlier. But the quality common to all representations of the word "brocade," is that they can all be factual representations. Non-factual associations may be among these, but the primary representations are concrete and refer to specifics. The word "honour" does not have this prerogative. Its first line of representations would be nonfactual and almost exclusively associational, useless for analytic purposes.

Why is Pope making this category mistake? With as careful a language user as Pope, it is not accidental. He seems rather, to be exploiting the possibilities of category mistakes, to see the effect he can obtain from them. (He is doing this exploiting, of course, in an age which didn't have to concern itself with the possible analytic pitfalls of such a course.) The effect he obtains is clearly brilliant. Not only does the juxtaposition show the range of concerns that occupy Belinda and company, but it also shows the similar value she accords honor and brocades, hearts (the seats of emotions) and necklaces. The same verbs used in both cases show us the superficial and grosso modo undiscriminating nature of a society's concern with appearances. A large chunk of social criticism couched in a category mistake.

The last thing to be said in this connection involves a
tiny subversion of the language analysts, or more exactly, their
reincorporation--death and transfiguration. We are acknowledging that Pope is making a category mistake here, and according
to the logical positivists, this is an incorrect use of language.
But in this case, the society that Pope is representing treats
these two logically incompatible pairs (honor-brocade, heart-
necklace) as equal in value. So, the most exact representation
of this society would be bound up in this "illogical" juxtaposition. This discovery creates a small dilemma. Do we criticize
Pope for the sake of linguistic logic, chastening our wayward
spirits but salving our conscience, or do we consider that the
first duty of a writer of manners and mores is accurate representation at any cost?

A giant, theoretical question like this which could under-
mine our entire thesis clearly cannot be given a simple, one-
line answer. Possible answers seem anyway to come in pairs,
and are linked with the perspective one wants to adopt. The
first pair: Can language be subject to inflexible laws according to which it must always act, or is it the flexible testimony to our social existence? The second pair, related to the
first: Is language a static entity that embodies in its very
existence all possibilities for discourse, or is its historically
effectual existence dependent on its ability to push its limits
further and further? These are the sorts of answers we want
to give to the question we raised, partially as hedging, but
also, because our entire thesis in this book is problematical.
We want to apply the work of the logical positivists to literature, because we feel that an incompatible position is often
most useful in getting literature on its haunches. But we're
not convinced that logical analysis is the nec plus ultra in
allowing literature to show off all it has. It seems rather

to put literature in the position of a burlesque queen in the
dark. We should keep some middleground position always somewhere in our critical consciousness, pushing language analysis
as far as it will go, but allowing it to bow out gracefully
when its concerns seem totally inappropriate to a particular
literary object. This may not happen too often. We may be
able to push analysis a surprising distance. That is, after
all, our orientation, and a preoriented point of view can move
mountains of syntax.

But is all syntax thus moveable? Let's look at a few lines
of a quite different sort. Belinda's lock has already been
spirited away by treachery, and she is determined to get it
back, severed as it is. So she appeals to her defender, Sir
Plume. His response is described:

> With earnest Eyes, and round unthinking Face
> He first the Snuff-box open'd, then the Case,
> And thus broke out--My Lord, why, what the Devil?
> Z--ds! damn the Lock! 'fore Gad, you must be
>   civil!
> Plague on't! 'tis past a Jest--nay prithee, Pox!
> Give her the Hair--he spoke, and rapp'd his Box.
> It grieves me much (reply'd the Peer again)
> Who speaks so well shou'd ever speak in vain.
> (IV,11.125-132)

It is apparent that Sir Plume doesn't speak well. In fact
he speaks very badly. Half his speech is execration, and the
other half is scarcely logical. So the peer's speech is ironic.
Our question here, and it belongs under the heading "the limits
of language analysis," is: could language analysis stricto sensu
demonstrate that the peer's words are ironic? The answer in a
word is, unlikely. Language analysis, with all its fruitful,
subtle concerns, somehow seems to lack a slot for irony. The
way language analysis looks at language presupposes intentions
that are pure and free of arrière pensée. Utterances may be confused, they may be misleading, using grammatical structures which

seem similar but are really different, or there may be other problems of a like nature, but duplicity is never assumed. In analytical terms, irony is a form of duplicity, since a sentence can be uttered in all the rigor of logical usage, but it will have a completely different intention.

It is difficult to think of a counter to this. Perhaps it exists in the realm of sense vs. denotation, or maybe even in associational thinking, where the object (here the sentence) carries with it a very different set of accidental meanings from that of the primary utterance. But even if we allow this explanation, we still have the problem of ascertaining the principal meaning of the ironic statement. It would have to be located in the literal meaning, for the associational thinking theory to be possible. Because associational thinking (object representations) concerns itself first with what is actually present in the words, and then with any chance secondary meaning.

In ironic language, what counts is usually the meaning strictly opposite to that of the literal meaning of the sentence. For an auditor or reader to understand correctly the sense of an ironic statement, he must be able to make a mental adjustment which is extra-linguistic; his interpretation must be there to complete the sense of the statement. The auditor's cue to make such an adjustment is the tone in which a statement is uttered, and tone is rather ephemeral for logical positive ears. It is sub-linguistic or super-linguistic, depending upon whether our orientation is animal or human, scientific or belletristic. But it anyway doesn't enter into syntactical considerations. And for the reader as opposed to the auditor, tone doesn't help at all. What does help, though, is context. In the Pope example with Sir Plume, knowing the context seemed essential to understanding the irony of the Baron's words. And if not the context, at least the surrounding sentences. Looking at the Baron's statement in itself tells us nothing, whatever tests we subject it to.

Irony is literature's tiny wedge against positivism; using it, literature can force positivism to seek solutions within literature itself, because the analytic formulae will just bounce off the edge.

iv

The closest logical analysis comes to acknowledging non-literal language use is in that connected with emotive statements, which can sometimes be translated by rephrasing into what they really mean. The Carnap example in Chapter I dealt with ethical statements, which are singled out because of the prominent part ethics plays and has played in the history of traditional philosophy. But ethical statements in Carnap's sense are really a special case of emotive statements in general, and these emotive statements are or should be subject to similar modifications.

Pope makes a number of emotive or ethical statements in The Rape of the Lock which we might examine to see if language analysis can help us sharpen them. The first one we'll look at is the point in the poem where Belinda is about to lose at cards:

> At this, the Blood the Virgin's Cheek forsook,
> A livid Paleness spreads o'er all her Look;
> She sees, and trembles at th' approaching Ill,
> Just in the Jaws of Ruin, and Codille.
> (III,1.89-92)

We might ask here if this is a true picture of emotion, or to put it another way, is the language acting in a representational capacity. We get more mileage from phrasing the question this second way, because for linetoeing Vienna Circlers, emotions don't really tell us about the world. Being a true picture of an emotion, would be like drawing a true picture of a dream. We might object here that emotions are much more "real" and substantial than dreams, being phenomena that can be experienced by more than one person at a time. But that leads us to Wittgenstein and private language, which would complicate matters at this point.

For the moment, we'll just look at the lines to see how representationally true they are, taking emotion here as an actual fact of existence: Blood forsaking a cheek, and being succeeded by paleness, are certainly possible physical events, although their origin need not be excessive emotion; it could also be excessive application of leeches. And seeing and trembling are also recordable phenomena. But after that everything changes. "Cheek" may mean something in itself, but "Virgin's Cheek" has no real meaning. "Virgin" is a connotative word, and although it refers to Belinda in this poem, it in general does not refer to an individual, but rather to a state common to many individuals. (The Virgin Mary is a prototype of the loss of denotation associated with a word's turning into an epithet. Belinda joins a long line of virgins in assuming it, but loses some more personal characteristics as a consequence. Pope, with his cynicism, would undoubtedly agree that "virgin" is sometimes a smokescreen. His use of the term "honour" confirms this.) "Look" in the line, "A livid Paleness spreads o'er all her Look," is another meaningless word here, but meaningless for a different reason. The word "look" has a function--as a maintainer of rhyme and rhythm, but it is meaningless in that it doesn't tell us any more about Belinda. Semantically, it doesn't add anything to the sentence. It is an insubstantial word, functioning like the word "aura," for example. Both are metaphysical terms, seemingly charged with deep meaning, but the precise significance of either can only be hinted at, which, from the positivist standpoint, means senselessness.

We have just a few more things to point to, after which Pope may wish he'd never written this poem. One of our questions is whether or not "Jaws of Ruin" has any meaning. Even looking closely, we find it hard to begin to describe what "in the Jaws of Ruin" might mean. "Jaws" is clear and needs no exegesis. And "Ruin," though vague in the sense that it can refer to something concrete, like, "The birthday cake is ruined," or something more abstract like, "he was ruined by wild speculation," has a meaning of sorts. But the complex, "Jaws of Ruin," seems highly improbable. One can imagine a Captain Ahablike situation for which the expression would be agreeably apt, but aside from something that fortuitous, the words in combination have no cognitive meaning.

A disjunction between literal and metaphorical meaning is particularly visible in this poem, where the type of image is so much at variance with the actual events that occur. Almost every part of the poem is in one way or another a battle description: preparations, combat, or aftermath. And the way Pope sustains the battle metaphor in the application of cosmetics, or in a game of cards, is a recognized tour de force, a triumph in the wielding of category mistakes. "Jaws of Ruin" seems a little weak, in the face of martial successes like, "Draw forth to Combat on the Velvet Plain" (referring to a baize card table), "The Baron now his Diamonds pours apace," or, "Th'inferior Priestess, at her Altar's side, / Trembling, begins the sacred Rites of Pride." Perhaps Pope's strength here does not lie in the evocation or representation of emotion. Other passages that deal with emotions are even more stylized than the one cited above. For example after Belinda's loss of hair, a gnome goes to the Goddess of Spleen to attempt the rousing of Belinda from her sunken state:

> A wondrous Bag with both her Hands
>   she binds,
> Like that where once Ulysses held
>   the winds;
> There she collects the Force of
>   Female Lungs,
> Sighs, Sobs, and Passions, and the
>   War of Tongues.
> A Vial next she fills with fainting
>   Fears,
> Soft Sorrows, melting Griefs, and
>   flowing Tears.
>   (IV,11.81-86)

There is nothing in all of this that even pretends to realism. It is really a mythical "explanation" of the manifestations of grief, heralded by an allusion to Ulysses and his wind bag. There is no attempt here to convince us that what is being described has any real phenomenal status. But there is a kind of concretizing one doesn't see every day. Emotions are not being shown as the ephemera we usually consider them, such that we have to spend millions of dollars training psychiatrists to recognize the faintest stirrings of the fragile psyche. These emotions (or their external manifestations) seem curiously real, within the mythical framework. They are present to us in almost the way Zeus's malevolence was present to the Greeks during thunderstorms. It is the sort of cause-and-effect explanation of emotion which even the language analysts might smile benignly on.

What we are saying is that the language here is not of the sort to evoke pathos because of the aptness of its representational qualities. In that sense it is unreal. But it is real, or effective, in the sense of our having objects to look at, procedures that are taking place. Of course, the price of this objectification is that these "objects" are rather indiscriminately mixed. Tears, sorrows, fainting fears, the war of tongues are all thrown together in a juxtaposition sustained only by

rhyme and meter. The specific density of each item is somewhat
blurred in this medley. Pope finally gains a small triumph,
because the chaos of this mixture resembles the disorder of persons (here women) thrown into an emotional state, a form of
representation after all. But this seems only perceptible after
we have worked through the anti-representational nature of these
lines.

It is easy to see why the logical positivists allude to
emotive utterances, but for the most part leave them alone,
after consigning them to the realm of metaphysics. Emotive
statements are a bit less malign in logical terms than pure
metaphysical philosophies, because while these philosophies foist
on innocent mankind a series of purposeful but senseless statements, emotive utterances are much less organized and operate
in a foggy, confused area without doctrine. Ethical statements
seem the bastard offspring of both schools. They are doctrinal
to the extent that they advocate certain ways of thinking about
human behavior. But, as Carnap has shown, they are essentially
emotional in the way they seek to influence behavior and thereby
implement certain wishes. The fact that they have this doctrinal
side to them makes ethical statements somewhat easier to examine
than other emotive statements. With ethical statements, we do
not worry about representational validity, as we have with other
forms of emotive statements. Ethical statements are given up
to their message, and to those few trappings which make these
statements a saleable package.

Pope, true to his Augustan _dulce et utile_ heritage, uses
The Rape of the Lock partially as a vehicle for making ethical
statements. One would imagine this would be hard to do in a
mock-epic, which, in all decorum, is not to be read with the
greater seriousness accorded an epic. But on the other hand,
serious statements are much more easily swallowed when couched

in comedy. Moralistic angularities have been rubbed smooth
and are accepted with a good will--a crackpot in a candy factory.

Pope begins the poem with a moralistic epic echo from
the Iliad: "What dire offence from am'rous Causes springs, /
What mighty Contests rise from trivial Things, / I sing . . ."
(I,11.1-3). While these thoughts were surely more than that
for Iliad hearers, to us they are a form of truism. That is
to say, they are something to be examined closely to see if
they are not true on borrowed time only, or borrowed fame.
In this case it is a little of both, and with enough vagueness
thrown in to make the statement absolutely unverifiable, in
experimental terms. So-called truisms are often of this
nature--large, grammatically plausible statements with no
pointers attached, no built-in means of acknowledging or refuting
them, short of discarding the entire statement as vague or meaningless. Here, the statements are meaningful only to the extent that they introduce a particular account that can be considered a particular case.

In Canto III, just before the cutting of the lock, there
is another flurry of moral statements: "Ah cease rash Youth!
desist ere 'tis too late, / Fear the just Gods, and think of
Scylla's Fate! (11.121-22), or, "But when to Mischief Mortals
bend their Will, / How soon they find fit Instruments of Ill!"
(11.125-6).

There are two kinds of moral statements here. The first
is monitory and is in the imperative. The other is descriptive
and makes an observation about the human condition. The first
statement is concerned with averting an event which has not yet
happened, but which has a precedent in epic history. Two different arguments are being brought into play here, although
they seem like the same one, because they share the imperative

form. "Fear the just Gods" is a very general admonishment,
having the same ethical value as "Be good!" but not the same
simplicity. "Fear the just Gods" is ambiguous (something to
be avoided in an ethical statement), because it can either mean,
"Fear only those gods who are just," or, "Fear the gods, all of
whom are by nature just." Apart from this complication, "Fear
the just Gods" is simply the expression of a wish that peoples'
behavior be in accordance with certain precepts, the observance
of which makes their actions of the sort termed "God-fearing"
by certain moralists. Again, we are dealing with a very loose,
rangy concept, one whose subheadings can be filled in in any
number of ways by any number of people, and which is therefore
not really a concept at all, according to some theories.

The second part of that same line--" . . . and think of
Scylla's Fate!" is a different sort of imperative. It bids the
listener to do one specific action, in this case, to remember a
particular story out of Greek mythology. (Scylla cut her father's
source of power, his hair, in a treacherous act which eventually
reduced her to a small sea bird.) Listeners obeying this in-
junction (presuming they are learned enough or have good enough
memories) will be rewarded by a foresight of a possible result
of their actions (or the type of this result, since the circumstances differ). "Fear the just Gods" is certainly qualified
by thinking about Scylla, because we know for what reason they
are to be feared. But the two imperatives are not parallel.
Both are implicit moral statements, but the one really says
nothing more (or less) than "live a good life," "be a moral
person," etc., while the other recommends the avoidance of an
"historically-demonstrated" unsavory course of action. (The
distinction between "be sagacious," and "think about all your
deductions" is worth remembering the next time you fill out a
tax form.)

"But when to Mischief Mortals bend their Will, / How soon
they find fit Instruments of Ill," is no longer in the heyday
of prescriptive statements. Dark shadows have fallen across
the paths of Virtue, and small, God-fearing footsteps have long
been obliterated. A veritable Götterdämmerung accompanies this
other breed of moral statement, which throws up its hands
Cassandralike, at the evil it can foresee but not prevent.
This statement is purely descriptive, and doesn't seek to change
actions directly. It just comments sadly on them, in a tone
which speaks of inevitability and universal truth. This line
has the same affective force as the above-mentioned, "What dire
offence from am'rous Causes springs," etc. It also has the
same non-specific quality about it.

An even more striking example of the very general nature
of most moral statements occurs toward the end of the poem, as
a rationalizing aftermath of the lock's being cut:

> How vain are all these Glories, all
>   our Pains,
> Unless good Sense preserve what
>   Beauty gains; . . .
> Oh, if to dance all Night, and dress
>   all Day,
> Charm'd the Small-pox, or chas'd old
>   Age away;
> Who would not scorn what Huswife's
>   Cares produce,
> Or who would learn one earthly Thing
>   of Use?
> To patch, nay ogle, might become a
>   Saint,
> Nor could it sure be such a Sin to
>   paint.
>
>   (V,11.15-24)

"Unless good Sense preserve what Beauty gains" is one of those
lines without a real subject. It has a grammatical subject
(we're ignoring the fact that this is a clause, not a complete
sentence). But as something concrete and capable of conscious

action, 'good sense' fails utterly. 'Good sense' by itself,
and as a quality, has never preserved anything, nor could it.
A person acting in a prudent manner, and thus demonstrating
good sense, might perhaps preserve something, but never good
sense alone. And while we're on the subject, the phrase 'good
sense' is itself rather vague, even after we have disbarred it
from active participation in life. One man's good sense is
another man's folly, and that sort of discrepancy holds for
beauty and virtue as well, big favorites with the ethical crowd.
The logical positivists are very hard on people who use these
terms in anything that resembles a defining spirit, and it is
easy to see why. But it is also easy to see the temptation these
words stir in each new human generation, causing its members to
speculate with assiduity on the life-defining possibilities of
these words. The fact that words like these are vague and lack
a specific denotation makes them seem capable of sustaining a
wider conceptual field. Anything (within certain limits) can
be substituted for them without changing the context. This is
why the words are favored by many but shunned by purists as
meaningless placeholders.

One can see the difficulty with this language even in the
poem. The big moral catch-alls are used repeatedly, but it is
hard even to ascertain their referents. What, for example,
does "beauty" mean in the poem? If there is any pivotal axis
here, it is something like beauty--virtue; attractiveness--good
sense. In other words, there is an implicit split between so-
called "moral" qualities (virtue) and other qualities which
might be considered "accidents of birth" or "exploitation of
natural advantages." (It is evidently more difficult to sub-
sume these latter qualities under a single heading because they
are even more polymorphous than the "moral" qualities, being
ways of circumventing these moral qualities.) At any rate, a

rough alignment of these two kinds of concerns is one way to
talk about the poem. But anything more than superficial observation of the poem reveals how inexactly these terms are used,
and how finally difficult it is even to place them in the right
relationships.[13] Where, for example, do we situate beauty?
Is it in Belinda's unadorned face? Is it rather Belinda after
the cosmetic scene ("Now awful Beauty puts on all its Arms"
(I,1.139)? Or is it rather beauty as a desideratum, beauty of
the soul, spiritual beauty? Beauty as an ensnarement is certainly a motif of the poem, but it is very hard to know who is
finally ensnared, the Baron, Belinda herself, or both. Sometimes
beauty is concretized in a single object, as the discursus on
hair in Canto II demonstrates:

> This Nymph, to the Destruction of
>   Mankind,
> Nourished two Locks, which grace-
>   ful hung behind . . .
> Love in these Labyrinths his Slaves
>   detains,
> And mighty Hearts are held in slender
>   Chains.
> With hairy Sprindges we the Birds
>   betray,
> Slight Lines of Hair surprize the
>   Finny Prey,
> Fair tresses Man's Imperial Race
>   insnare,
> And Beauty draws us with a single
>   Hair.
>   (11.19-28).

As the last line of this shows, hair has really become beauty,
or vice-versa. So while hair does the trapping of such lowlifes

---

[13]The situating of large terms like these along thematic
axes is a favorite technique of the structuralists, who do not
always realize the actual vagueness of the terms used. The
insights furnished by language analysis might not be amiss here.

as fish or birds, beauty as hair waylays presumably higher-mettled objects like human hearts.

Although identified with hair, beauty as a distinct image collapses even here. Pope is using a really skillful scintillation effect in this passage, with the alternance and merging of hair and beauty to the point where we ourselves see no way out of the linguistic trap. This technique works very well in poetry, but doesn't give language analysts anything to hold on to. It cannot but confirm their fears about the ambiguity of abstract terms. A possible way around this awful verdict would be to appeal to sense and denotation reasoning--that beauty is the denotation and all these variants are different senses of beauty, different ways we have of talking about it. It would be hard to argue with this explanation, except to say that "beauty" is too abstract even to have a denotation.

V

In a perfect language, the word "beauty" would mean one thing and one thing only. Or else each separate sense or occurrence of beauty would have its own, unambiguous word, like what the Greeks were tending toward in having three words to describe the different types of love, or like what the Laps have probably succeeded in, with forty different ways of saying "snow." Whether it is better to have one word refer to one specific quality, or twenty words for different aspects of that quality, is debatable. It depends a little on how a culture perceives the world, what aspects of the world present themselves as more worthy of notice. A perfect language is in a way more a philosophical ideal than a ceiling of language attainment, because there is an enormous tension between just how precise language can be about objects, and the possibilities for communication.

Wittgenstein, in the Tractatus, alludes to the difficulty
of generalizing about objects: "Roughly speaking, to say of
two things that they are identical is nonsense, and to say of
one that it is identical with itself is to say nothing at all."[14]
If one fox is not identical with another, then why do they both
have the same name? Wittgenstein could easily destroy the world,
having done away with the concept of identity, which seems funda-
mental. Almost every thinking being has some recourse to this
concept, whether to identify his family members (as opposed to
another family), or to go to his job on Tuesday, assuming he
will be doing the same thing as on Monday, etc. Even our ability
to reason with any coherence seems based on the fact that past
experiences are the type of future ones. And much training of
young children and animals is based on an identical response to
the same blandishment. Yet it is true that in strictly analytic
terms, one chair is different from another, even though the two
look the same. And ideally, this fact should be accounted for.

Let's suppose a language in which this specificity is
given full rein. I have two trees in my yard, both Mimosas.
Since they can't be identical, one is called kirg and the other,
mrush. My neighbor has an enormous plot of land, on which are
growing fifty mimosas, each of course different. The first on
the left side of the first row is called hurg, the second, braf,
the third, yaup, etc. Suppose my neighbor says to me one day,
"I need to cut down the swarch today." (The definite article
is present because these are not names, but type designations.)
"Could you please leave your hatchet beside it when you leave
for work." Unless I have put in full time getting acquainted
with my neighbor and his trees, I probably won't know which

---

[14]Ludwig Wittgenstein, Tractatus Logico-Philosophicus
(London 1961) p. 105.

tree he is referring to, and he might never find my hatchet,
or grizz, depending upon which he wants to borrow.

This illustration doesn't really prove anything, unfortunately. Because in order to demonstrate the difficulty of applying this specific terminology to the world of objects, we
have first to generalize about these objects, in order to show
what we are departing from. For example, in such a system,
neither I nor my neighbor would know that the trees were all
called "mimosas." We would be able to differentiate a mimosalike
tree from a hatchet, but we wouldn't know it was a mimosa we
were differentiating. Besides that, there would have to be almost an infinite number of words to designate all the objects
in the world. And it would be a rare person who knew what even
a thousandth of them referred to. In effect, without the help
and shortcuts furnished by the generalizing tendencies in language, communication might break down entirely.

But perhaps a society that talked about objects with this
particularity would die out of its own accord, because the question of the use of each object would have to be considered.
If one hatchet seemed different from another, and each had a
different designation, then how would we know that they both
could chop down trees? And how would we know, if we ate a particular berry from a bush with no ill effects, that a second
one from the same bush would not be fatal? The possibilities
for caricature of a presumptive society like this are as endless as the number of objects in the world, but even imagining
living in such a society is impossible. Without certain subsuming concepts, so many ways of talking about things that we
take for granted would be eliminated a priori.

The famous joke about all Asians' looking alike to non-
Asians (and probably vice-versa) is likely to have more truth
in it than is generally admitted in cautious, non-racist

statements. Unfamiliarity, which at its most perceptive merely notices, makes it impossible really to distinguish; we are presented with a sudden blast of unconquered material, for which we don't have a pre-established slot, and for instant survival, we think, "that's different from us" (understood "it's all the same in its differentness from us"). On longer acquaintance, of course, the differences are more readily perceptible, once the initial, threatening, totalizing difference has been accounted for.

It would seem then, that the initial way of perceiving the world (for the infant who knows only self and other, for the student of Linnean classification) would be a generalizing way, quite unlike my neighbor with the mimosas. Which is of course an exaggerated example. But it shows the necessity of having generalizing concepts (and with them certain regularly satisfied expectations) in order for existence to proceed with any semblance of fluidity and continuity.

vi

It is often mentioned that art is the way to restore particularity to the objects we have deprived of it through conceptualizing. There seems to be much merit to this statement, which applies of course to the graphic and plastic arts as well as to literature. If there were one hundred different people writing a poem on the same object, it is highly unlikely that any two poems would be identical. Each poem would have a particular slant, would point to certain aspects of the object to the neglect of others. And one poem-writer reading another's poem might well be surprised at what appeared worthy of comment and observation to the other. The infinite variety of human thought could be celebrated here, but we'd rather point to the

necessarily partial view of phenomena which is the only one
art permits. That is the price of particularity.

But it is also the false comfort of concepts. Why false?
Well, for one thing, because concepts themselves are shorthand
forms, cartes blanches for not thinking details out completely,
for not enumerating components. (Notice the use of "carte
blanche" in the preceding sentence.) And even where such an
attempt at saturation is made, as in the case of semiological
studies of individual words, the conceptual foundations are not
always reached.

Any meaningful word is capable of being broken down into
its "sèmes," or smaller meaning units. The sèmes of the word,
"clothing," for example, might be "protective garments," "or-
namental covering," etc. "Chair" might have as sèmes, "Structure for sitting," "made of wood," "composed of two more-or-less
perpendicular parts and four supports for these two parts," etc.
But as Oswald Ducrot points out,

> Comment reconnaître alors si une unité
> linguistique comme "homme"--nous parlons
> du signifié de la langue française et
> non pas du concept de la classification
> zoologique--comporte les deux sèmes
> "animal" + "raisonnable" ou les deux
> sèmes "bipède" + "sans plume"? Comment
> déterminer aussi s'il faut analyser
> "savoir", et y trouver les sèmes
> "croyance" + "vérité de cette croyance",
> et, dans ce cas, comment décider si le
> sème "croyance" contenu dans "il sait"
> est identique à celui qu'on peut
> déceler dans "il s'imagine", etc.[15]

So even with the best of analytic intentions, it is difficult
to know just what particulars stand at the base of concepts (or

---

[15]Oswald Ducrot, Qu'est-ce que le structuralisme? I. Le
Structuralisme en linguistique (Paris 1968) p. 63.

even of other particulars). Particulars seem to have a life of
their own, occasionally submitting themselves to forming a substratum of concepts, at other times remaining obdurate and unin-
corporable. This tough area is perhaps the realm of art, where
objects (particulars) exist in a state somewhere between "an sich"
and "giving testimony of the world." Concepts embody neither of
these poles, except to the extent that they are composed of objects. And we have seen how difficult that relation is to pin-
point. We looked at the various ways one can reduce the concept
of man into its constituents. If we want to regard the concept
of man as something featherless or something reasonable, we have
to make a perceptual choice, and different objects will be entailed
in our choice. Semiologists and builders of conceptual systems
have to worry about their preordained defeat at the hands of the
arbitrary, which is system's prime enemy. Art takes the arbitrary
as its religion, makes a system of nonsystem, writes a poem about
"the concept of man."

> There Affectation with a sickly Mien
> Shows in her Cheek the Roses of
>   Eighteen,
> Practis'd to Lisp, and hang the Head
>   aside,
> Faints into Airs, and languishes with
>   Pride;
> On the rich Quilt sinks with becoming
>   Woe,
> Wrapt in a Gown, for Sickness, and for
>   Show.
> The Fair-ones feel such Maladies as
>   These,
> When each new Night-Dress gives a new
>   Disease.
>   (IV,31-8)

There is a kind of concept, or conceit in these lines, which is
of course affectation. We also have a display of the components
of affectation, which, within the frame of the poem, answers the
question, "What is affectation?" Affectation, here, is the figure

of a woman who demonstrates to an exaggerated extent a number of
feminine mannerisms. The concept of affectation is thus shown
to be composed of particulars, some of which are themselves other
concepts. For example, "shows in her Cheek the Roses of Eighteen"
suggests not only the bright color of her cheek, but all the
other youthful, burgeoning, fertile qualities that endow this
concept with affective life. The other, more well-known components of affectation are also in evidence, like lisping, hanging
the head, fainting. (Since affectation is a peculiarly good index of the particular manner of an epoch, these gestures might
be expected to change with the century. This is eighteenth ·
century affectation.) In some ways this enumeration of the qualities that might be subsumed under the term, "affectation" is no
different from breaking down the concept in any non-literary
analytic way, like giving a dictionary definition.

But art leaves its own stamp. It is giving a definition,
but it's in the form of an example. And the example is, as any
college freshman knows, an allegory, the picture of a woman
whose whole life is given up to affectation, is affectation.
Only rarely have concepts such a sensuous embodiment outside the
arts. For literature, allegory is the perfect vehicle for ex-
plaining a concept and giving it life and plastic form at the
same time. That is why allegory is frequently employed for di-
dactic purposes (which, we must admit, are not strictly part of
concepts).

Up to this point we have been more or less following the
idea that literature confers particularity to concepts. And with
this goes the implicit view that this particularity is necessarily partial, due to concentration on smaller aspects, and therefore somehow inexact. But in the case of allegory, there seems
to be a built-in corrective to an overly partial point of view.
In allegory, the possibilities for a microcosmic presentation of

reality are greatly facilitated by the constant presence of fig-
ures with names like Sin, Vanity, Prudence, etc. The concept is
never really left behind. Descriptions of particulars are in-
evitable, but they are constantly being justified and checked
against the whole, which needs to be completed and fleshed out
for any of the particulars to make sense. The process is dialectical, because the particulars in themselves, without reference
to the allegorical concept, are meaningless as linguistic signs
pointing toward a completion. And the concept too, without
particulars to give it life and a form, is barren and even self-
annihilating.

Take our example of Affectation. If she had only a 'sickly
Mien,' or only 'the Roses of Eighteen,' there would be nothing
to distinguish her from any other young lady given to spleen or
choler. But the combination of these characteristics, which don't
ordinarily go together, makes us suspect there is something special in this description, something afoot. And then when we add
the other qualities, like 'practis'd to Lisp' and hanging of the
head, we begin to see a sort of behavioral consistency in this
young lady. (One doesn't normally practice lisping; it comes
naturally, or not at all.) Our conviction about contradictory
poses is almost completely seconded by, 'Faints into Airs, and
languishes with Pride,' because these responses are indeed inappropriate. And phrases like 'becoming Woe,' and, 'For Sickness
and for Show,' complete even more explicitly our impression of
this Living Lie.

The approach to an allegorical figure is accretive;
enough particulars are required for the concept to emerge from
the block of marble, but past a certain point, they become
mutually confirmatory and self-justifying. Exactly where that
point is is difficult to say, just as one can never feel absolutely confident about having analyzed a concept to the farthest

reaches of its semantic borders. But the argument that art only
presents us with a partial view of reality, and that concepts
are more general, is somewhat qualified (not dispelled) by remembering the resources art has available to it, like allegory.

vii

Related to the question of concepts and their constituent
objects (or sometimes, constituent concepts) is the subject of
sense and denotation in literary language. Here, the emphasis
shifts to the many possible ways of describing an object. In
other words, instead of "simply" trying to peer into the entrails
of a concept, we want to take a concept and make it an icon, put
it at a distance and show the various approaches to it. In
literature, this is a sort of language game--displaying the
agility of language by indicating an object in more than one way.
But for the language analysts, this is serious business. Naming
the possibilities for multiple description of a word or concept
is a way to be on the alert for possible ambiguities in usage
which occur in spite of logical rules of discourse. So littera-
teurs and language analysts come upon the phenomenon of different ways of pointing at something with feelings that could not
be described as identical.

Pope does not hesitate to appear polysemous in this way.
In fact he rather basks in the murkiness of the whole illicit
procedure, of making language do what God didn't intend it to
do. As the reader has probably already surmised, this is about
the time for an illustrative passage:

> Not youthful Kings in Battel seiz'd
>   alive,
> Not scornful Virgins who their Charms
>   survive,
> Not ardent Lovers robb'd of all their
>   Bliss,
> Not ancient Ladies when refus'd a Kiss,

> Not Tyrants fierce that unrepenting die,
> Not <u>Cynthia</u> when her Manteau's pinn'd
>   awry,
> E'er felt such Rage, Resentment and
>   Despair,
> As Thou, sad Virgin! for thy ravish'd
>   Hair.
>   (IV,11.3-10)

There are a lot of lines here that begin with "not." And they
all refer to seemingly different things, like spurned old ladies,
captive kings, despoiled lovers. But--and here there is a significant pause--there is a common element somewhere. And that
element is rage. All these 'nots' are different ways of talking about rage. (Eureka!) In effect, the denotation is rage,
and these 'not' lines are different senses of it (remember morning
star and evening star). Is this then, a way of confusing us as
to the 'real' meaning of rage? On the contrary, it seems to be
an amplification of the concept, a way of bringing the meaning
of rage home to the reader whose range of emotions is only mid-
dling. At least one of these senses of rage is bound to engage
most readers, at the best, through some direct experience that
preceded the reading of the poem, or more realistically, through
having read about such instances in other literature. (Inciden-
tally, neither of these ways of connecting with the term 'rage'
would be of any interest to the logical positivists, 1) because
reading is not the same thing as having a direct experience of
a thing, 2) even a direct experience of something like rage would
not constitute proof, that such an experience would ever be repeated, although there might be some likelihood, and primarily,
3) because rage as an emotion suffers inherently from a lack of
verification possibilities, and is therefore of no genuine interest to the positivists.) With these objections duly recorded,
we want to say that the existence of rage says something about
the human condition, stretches some thread more fully, and is to

that extent a datum of the phenomenal world. We do not want to say that we can always gauge its extent, or even describe it accurately. The "nots" in the cited lines show how complex its manifestations can be, and convince us that we need the various senses of the term, all of which add to it, but none of which complete it.

It might complicate things at this point to speak of the humor in these lines of Pope, but we would not be doing the language justice if we didn't at least mention it. The various nots can in themselves be viewed as cases in point of rage, but the juxtaposition of 'Youthful Kings in Battel seiz'd alive,' with 'ancient Ladies when refus'd a Kiss' cannot help but suggest a comic perspective for all of this. As we tried to show earlier in terms of style, this is mock-epic, and the swoop from sublime to ridiculous leads to humor, as well as gives Pope a chance to talk about eighteenth-century mores in a more timeless framework, that of epic historicity. Juxtaposition of this sort leads inevitably to differences in texture which feel like different degrees of realism. "Tyrants" seem like more of an abstraction than "ancient Ladies," although both exist and will continue to exist. But it is not often that the two find themselves sharing the same corner of poetry. Thanks to Pope and language analysis, ancient ladies and tyrants meet for the first time on truly logical grounds, where before, it was all exploitation and recriminations.

viii

Although Frege doesn't make this particular distinction, we feel like saying that there seems to be more than one type of manifestation of the sense and denotation complex. The one we looked at concerned itself with the term "rage" and displayed a number of senses of that word. But Pope elsewhere approaches the sense and denotation distinction in another way. (More accurately, we can see in certain of Pope's lines another application of a different kind of sense and denotation question. In this sort of analytical writing, temporal distinctions tend to flatten out, and one finds oneself ascribing to the author of a poem consciousness of critical theories he could never possibly have had. It is a pernicious disease, this "critical contagion" and authors of primary texts should be wary of it, and build into their writing some booby traps.)[16]

These much-heralded lines are the following:

> There broken Vows, and Death-bed Alms
>   are found,
> And Lover's Hearts with Ends of Riband
>   bound;
> The Courtier's Promises, and Sick Man's
>   Pray'rs,
> The Smiles of Harlots, and the Tears of
>   Heirs,
>
> (V,1.117-120).

The common element to this collection of objects is not immediately apparent. If we look at the literal meaning of the lines, we find only a series of paired nouns, most of which deal with emotions of some sort. But if we look at the particular nouns that form each pair, we find a sort of relationship that is sustained in almost every case. What is the shared element in the prayers of a sick man and the tears of heirs? Well, among other things, they are both in extremis situations. But then, what about the courtier's promises, or the smiles of harlots? In extremis flies out the window, and is replaced by falsity, or insincerity. And if we look at the group of nouns, we find that falsity or insincerity applies to all of them. Does falsity then stand in the same relation to these lines, that rage did to the earlier ones? Yes

---

[16]Like footnotes saying, "I knew you'd fall for that."

and no. Yes, because all the noun groups are ways of demonstrating falsity. But no, because falsity is not the literal meaning
of the lines. The 'smiles of Harlots' simply means a type of
facial expression that women in a certain profession sometimes
assume. And 'Death-bed alms' most likely means charity that is
given at the time of dying (although 'death-bed' is an elliptical
expression here). But the associations are much too cynical and
striking to stop at the literal meaning of any of these pairs.
We all know that eighteenth-century "women of the night" smiled
with much calculation, and that the smile widened with additional
shillings. And we know also, that alms at the time of dying have
a particular motivation which is rarely that of altruism. In the
same spirit, classic heirs seldom cry for the loss of the de-
ceased's company, never more to see his radiant face at the sup-
per board. And so on. In each noun-pair there is a distinction
between the denotation, or literal meaning, and the sense, or
extended figurative meaning. In the rage example, there was no
such split between the literal and ironic meanings of the lines.
There, all lines pointed to rage, whereas here, all lines point
to a superlinguistic meaning cluster which surrounds and completes the literal meaning.

ix

Acknowledging the fact that the sense of a word or phrase
occasionally differs from its denotation, seems to be a way of
saying that language use sometimes differs from its intention.
This realization accompanies the general shift in emphasis among
linguists from language as representation to language as communication. Earlier, we discussed some of the difficulties of presenting language as a picture of reality. Except for certain
onomatopoetic words (and their actual resemblance to phenomena is
suspect), it is difficult to sustain any simpleminded, one-to-one

correspondence between words and things. It is much easier to
see language as a form of testimony to the social existence of
human beings, the behavior of whom is constantly being modified
by what is said to them. Possibilities for language are rede-
fined, and recreated, by the pulsing presence of other speech
machines, rather than the sterile presence of objective schemata.
Words and phrases constantly take on new senses, as language leaps
from what it is to represent, to what it must respond to. This
somewhat ecstatic view of language is not meant to take from it
its rightful place as the source and medium of this social ex-
change. Even in the Pope example, we can see the sense and denotation distinction as the ontology of one kind of social criticism. A reader's non-literal approach to these lines is essential if a genuine act of communication is to take place.

x

We discussed at some length the Wittgenstein section on
private language. That would be the implicit antithesis to language that is acting, responding, and changing in a social
milieu. Wittgenstein "concluded" (in quotation marks because he
doesn't really write in such a positivistic spirit) that a private language is impossible, because if it functions according
to the rules of other languages, it wouldn't really be private.
Even being able to describe such a language to oneself would in-
validate it, since it would be borrowing its descriptive possibilities from the metalanguage that governs the world. And being
unable to describe the language would be like seeing the face of
God and not returning alive--a metaphysics of the pantry.

The paradoxical impossibility of a private language in the
world of human discourse does not prevent our application of this
notion to literature and the speech of characters. It is like
swimming naked on private property--there is a protective

framework around a literary work as created object that gives it
laissez-faire to speak in any way that furthers its purposes.
Private language can always then refer back to the fact that it
is created language, that someone created it, so that in some
sphere it is not really private. That approach would not violate
Wittgenstein's thesis. But let's look at a few passages from
Pope, to see if literary private language is really as simple as
all that.

The first example is from Canto II, and the context is self-
explanatory:

> Th' Adventrous Baron the bright Locks admir'd,
> He saw, he wish'd, and to the Prize aspir'd:
> Resolv'd to win, he meditates the way,
> By Force to ravish, or by Fraud betray;
> For when Success a Lover's Toil attends,
> Few ask, if Fraud or Force attain'd his Ends.
> (11.29-34).

This is a fairly simple example of private language, the sort
known to us via the mouths of every intriguer that ever walked
across a stage, or graced an epic poem. Either we have an 'I am
determined to prove a villain' Richard III, who tells the audience
his motives before he blurts them to anyone else, or someone like
the Baron who is meditating, and whom we see meditating. The
meditation taking place in the Baron's brain is still "private"
with respect to the other characters in the poem, who don't yet
know his plans, and it is even, to a certain extent, unknown to
us. Because while we know the gross choice he has to make--force
or fraud--we can't yet know the more precise working out of his
plot. And as the last two lines show, ('For when Success a Lover's
Toil attends, / Few ask, if Fraud or Force attain'd his Ends')
there may be a large space carved out that is to be even ultimately a private area. "Nothing succeeds like success" is the
crass, current day equivalent, which suggests in the same way the
sacrosanct space that comes in the train of every project whose

direction and result are known, but whose intermediate years of struggle are shrouded in Athena's mantle. For the Baron, discretion is further assured, in that we don't even know who these 'few' are, who would be maniacally curious enough really to want this explanation of method choice, superfluous as it now seems. Are these 'few,' other characters in the poem, who would seem to be the ones most concerned in retracing this triste histoire, or the morally conscientious reader, who wants a faithful rendition of the foibles of the human heart? Or is it simply a reference to the moral state of the outside world, whose nefarious private purposes are the model for the Baron's activities? A truly private purpose can't in actuality be a model for another one, for the same reason that a private language can't be described using the facilities furnished by a preexistent language. A suggestion of obscurity is probably all Pope is working towards here, with the implication that the reader who is faithfully following the argument of the poem will know in time.

This is a comparatively simple example of private language at work, but the ramifications, as we have seen, are rather farflung. Because private in anything but the icy-pure, sterilized Wittgenstein sense means, in effect, known to certain people and unknown to others. And this sort of epistemological ascertaining is difficult when we're considering a range from other characters in the same poem to readers of that poem. But that would be the range one would have to be concerned with, if the question of private language in literature is to be at all ontologically interesting.

A second example might extend that ontology. This passage occurs at a critical juncture of the poem, just a few lines before the cutting of the lock. It is a tension-fraught moment for the reader, and an even more excruciating time for the sylphs whose function it is to guard Belinda from harm. In short, everyone is waiting, except Belinda, who doesn't know about the proximity of the danger:

> Thrice she look'd back, and thrice
>   the Foe drew near.
> Just in that instant, anxious Ariel
>   sought
> The close Recesses of the Virgin's
>   Thought;
> As on the Nosegay in her Breast
>   reclin'd,
> He watch'd th' Ideas rising in her Mind,
> Sudden he view'd in spite of all her
>   Art,
> An Earthly Lover lurking at her Heart.
> Amaz'd, confus'd, he found his Pow'r
>   expir'd,
> Resign'd to Fate, and with a Sigh
>   retir'd.
>
>   (III,11.138-146)

Here we have an example of the kind of private language that permits us to feel we are in a privileged position. This feeling results partially from the fact that Belinda doesn't know what we, as readers, are seeing. And also from the making visible of things that are usually invisible, like sylphs and thought processes.

There are really then, a number of things going on here all at once, and it might be useful to number them: 1) Belinda is oblivious to the danger that threatens her; 2) Ariel remains alert to the danger and is trying to save her; 3) Ariel sees Belinda's thoughts; 4) Which thoughts are far from the present danger, and concern "an earthly lover" (who is unspecified but probably related to the "billet doux" of Canto I,1.118); 5) At the evidence of such a non-celestial concern, Ariel is confused and rendered impotent, and 6) The reader is able to observe all of the preceding.

It is evident in this section that of the four distinct personalities, Belinda, the Baron, Ariel, and the reader, each has a separate and thus "private" perspective. The Baron sees only Belinda (or more concretely Belinda's hair) as the object of desire and long planning. He doesn't know about the sylph, or the voyeuristic reader, and he doesn't know what Belinda is thinking. As for Belinda, lost in the steaming coffee as she is ("which makes the Politician Wise, / And see thro' all things with his half-shut Eyes"), she is unaware of the Baron's intentions, the sylph's vigilance (except for an annoying twitch at the ear once in a while) or the reader's abnormal interest. She does, however, know her own thoughts presumably better than anyone else except Pope, and that is debatable. Ariel has a somewhat wider view of things. As sylph, he is privileged to penetrate certain private areas that are unknown to others, like the substance of Belinda's thought, without himself being visible and accounted part of the picture. As such, he knows the Baron's intentions and Belinda's thoughts. But whether he knows any more than the gross substance of her thought, the 'earthly lover' that is, whether or not he can see the thoughts in detail, visualize them in some way, is unknown to us.

What precisely, is known to us here, as readers? We have first of all, a wider perspective than any of the characters, because we can see all of them. (Remember, no one else here can see the sylph.) So as we are watching all of this (and maybe idly wondering who is watching us), we are feeling sufficiently confident about our ontology with regard to these other beings. But how far does our knowledge extend? Do we know precisely the form the Baron's thoughts are taking at this moment? Not really. And how about the about-to-be-offended party's thoughts? Do we even know as much about them as the sylph does? Again, we must answer no. Doesn't this mean then, that in spite of our being

able to watch the scene, we remain comparatively ignorant? Yes,
interestingly enough.

Maybe being a reader isn't always the same thing as being
omniscient, with respect to a particular piece of literature.
The assertion could be made, that the only one who really knows
what Belinda is thinking is Belinda herself. We have to take the
sylph's word for it, that Belinda is having a series of thoughts,
one of which is about an unsavory earthly lover. But we can't
know what the sylph is seeing, exactly what the thought of an
earthly lover looks like. We're not even sure that Pope, although he created Belinda, can know what such a person's thoughts
look like. If Belinda is indeed having the thoughts ascribed to
her, then she, and she alone, would know the form they are taking. And if she doesn't know their form, then it can't be she
who is having the thoughts. On the other hand, if Pope created
Belinda, then he also created her thoughts. But did he or didn't
he create a Belinda who knows what she is thinking. That seems
to be the crux of the problem.

Maybe we should put the discussion in more general terms,
those of author, narrator, reader, and characters. What we're
wondering is whether there is any private area known to the characters of a literary work, which is not known to their author,
or to the reader. Innumerable critical studies, among them a
very clear-headed book like Wayne Booth's The Rhetoric of Fiction[17]
have dealt with questions concerning the narration of a literary
work. This is an endlessly teasing and suggestive area of interest, locating itself as it does at the borders of fiction and
reality. What a narrator tells us about a character, what he
leaves unsaid, whether or not he tells the truth, how much he
knows, and how he stands in relation to the author and characters,

---

[17]Wayne Booth, The Rhetoric of Fiction (Chicago 1961).

are only the outlines of a question which is truly complex, and which we, as readers, feel called upon to decide about so our own position doesn't become too uncomfortable. The problem of a private language for literary characters seems to be of a similar sort, partially a question of technique, partially a matter of almost pure speculation. It is in this spirit that we pursue the issue, knowing very well that we long ago lost the support, approval, and even interest of the language analysts (specifically Wittgenstein) by whom "private language" was first put forth as a topic.

Given the very modern (but also very seventeenth-century) notion that author and narrator are rarely, if ever, identical, but that a narrator is often (though not always) an author's _porte parole_, how are we to establish where the truth of any utterance is located? How are we to decide the precise way a statement is framed, and how qualify its literal meaning? And most of all, how are we to determine the extent of what each category of existent knows?

These are not the sort of questions one ordinarily hurries to answer, because they really have no answer that is objectively verifiable. Thinking about what a character might be thinking about seems the height of speculative folly, and surely the narrator created by an author is always under some sort of control. But then why use the technique of a narrator at all? Why not tell the story directly? Surely an author desires his fiction to have a certain amount of autonomy, something about it that makes it not simply an extension of the author. And once such an autonomous process is set into motion, it seems fair and even logical that one examine it on its own merits. A sort of argument in favor of this procedure is the obvious one that no matter what else is known about a literary work, a reader will never know definitively what an author is thinking, and the author will

similarly not know what his readers think, or even who they are.
Given the virtual mystery that surrounds the thoughts of these
two active participants in the literary game, it is surprising
that biographical studies that "reveal" the real meaning of a work
have been and continue to be welcomed as insightful. Acceptance
of such studies demonstrates a somewhat naive faith in determin-
istic, largely psychological "laws" of human behavior, which presuppose one possible sort of behavior from one sort of person.
Shrinking possibilities in this way is among the bleakest activities of literary analysts, one that leaves unreliable narrators
and glib-tongued characters with the undeniable feeling of being
de trop. Because a literary analysis whose focus is the life and
hard times of an author can't possibly be talking about the
author's work. No element of the work can be considered on its
own, when the search is aimed at resemblances and derivatives.

What if the narrator, for example, is very different from
the author, perhaps the sort of persona an author would like to
have, or not like to. Wouldn't the fact of this difference be
finally subsumed under one of many neo-Freudian sub-headings, to
be explained away motivationally at the reader's leisure? What
if we instead began by examining the speech of the characters,
or of the narrator, who is usually there, if only implicitly.
Wouldn't that be the way toward evolving a more functional theory
of the relationships among characters, and the ideas that seem to
be forming out of these relationships? Isn't Belinda entitled
to have her private thoughts, if what she expresses and what she
only suggests or even leaves unsaid are alike of significance to
the reader who regards literature as dynamic, and not something
about which all has long ago been said?

Certainly all never will be said, since much will be
thought. That is probably what Gilbert Ryle also concluded,
since he felt it worthwhile to create a theory of imaging as
part of his general interest in language analysis. We described
this theory in some detail in Chapter I. In very general terms,
the theory runs that people who hear a tune in their head, or
see a picture in their mind's eye, are not really hearing a
tune, or seeing a picture. This is true in spite of the fact
that the linguistic formulae we use for talking about these
phenomena are drawn from the world of physical seeing or hearing. According to Ryle, using one type of language for an area
of behavior that really demands another type, is one source
of the confusion.

This theory, combined with Wittgenstein's theory of private language, might be considered to be on the fringe of
positivistic thinking. As we have seen with private language,
both of these topics tread a narrow line between language analysis and metaphysics. Of course metaphysics is not the desired outcome of this kind of investigation, but rather exactitude of language use. The implicit idea is that sloppy habits
of speech are responsible for sloppy thinking. But once you
enter the realm of another's brain, even the most rigid lines   .
of thought tend to get warped, if not in the expository stage,
then at the level of demonstration. Even so, the topic seems
worth dealing with, since it is an attempt to analyze the imaginative process, of which literature is one of the demonstrable
results.

The highly fanciful nature of The Rape of the Lock encour-
ages us to look at it in terms of imaging. And as early as
Canto I, there is a violation of Ryle's dictional rules for
talking about the imagination:

> Then gay Ideas crowd the vacant Brain;
> While Peers and Dukes, and all their
>   sweeping Train,
> And Garters, Stars, and Coronets appear,
> And in soft sounds, Your Grace salutes
>   their Ear.
> 'Tis these that early taint the Female
>   Soul,
>
>   (11.83-87)

Can you find the mistake in these lines? It is the line, "Then gay Ideas crowd the vacant Brain." This line is doing just what Ryle wouldn't have wanted it to--implying that images are tangible and almost bodily enough to be able to 'crowd' a brain, like trying to fit too many pictures into a gallery. Picture gallery is, in fact, a metaphor that Ryle uses to demonstrate the type of wrong concept people have about imaging--that it is somehow physically present and potentially cumulative. That is the sort of mistake Pope is making here, although he does his best to fill his Ideas with substance (Peers, dukes, garters, sounds). Since this is poetry, we can justify the questionable nature of these 'Ideas' by saying they are metaphors, just as Garters and Stars are metaphors for Nobility, or for particular nobles. In this passage, the status of ideas is not properly located, as it would be in an actual thinking person. Ideas, garters, 'taints of the Female Soul,' all go together as tropes, not as describable epistemological processes. A narrow escape for Pope.

Since Pope, in common with many poets, feels the need to talk about the human soul, he has to resort from time to time to the world of imagination, which is Ryle's world too, for different reasons. Part of the joy of The Rape of the Lock is the familiarity Pope seems to have with the inner world of his characters, particularly the female characters. He delights in the contrast, both psychological and physical, between the

boudoir and the ballroom, the self in the making and the self
as finished product. Probably the only way to give a sense of
continuity to these presumably different states is via the imagination, by which a person shows himself to himself as he was,
or as he wants to be. This faculty was at work in Belinda during the cosmetic scene, which we alluded to earlier. It is also at work after her fall, after the lock has been cut. Imagination's surging at this time is understandable, in view of
the horror, chagrin, indignation, etc., the cutting of the hair
caused her. Pope doesn't waste the opportunity to give us a
look at Belinda's mind during this time:

> Was it for this you took such constant
>   Care
> The Bodkin, Comb, and Essence to pre-
>   pare;
> For this your Locks in Paper-Durance
>   bound,
> For this with tort'ring Irons wreath'd
>   around?
> For this with Fillets strain'd your
>   tender Head,
> And bravely bore the double Loads of
>   Lead?
> Gods! shall the Ravisher display your
>   Hair,
> While the Fops envy, and the Ladies
>   stare! . . .
> Methinks already I your Tears survey,
> Already hear the horrid things they
>   say,
> Already see you a degraded Toast,
> And all your Honour in a Whisper lost!
> $\qquad\qquad\qquad$ (IV,11.97-110)

We seem able to distinguish two different types of imaging occurring here: one that begins with the first line and
goes to "Methinks," and the other which extends to the end of
the passage. We might not have made this distinction if Ryle
had not previously sensitized us to subtleties of this sort.

Now, our point of view is tainted with discrimination. In any case, the first few lines are an example of the kind of imaging Ryle claims does not exist--that in which discrete pictures are presented to the self. As Belinda talks in a moralistic strain about the years of care lavished on her now-absent lock, she seems to be seeing vignettes of the various toilsome methods that force hair to look unnaturally natural (naturally unnatural?), the fillets, curlpapers, irons, all the cosmetic artillery. As readers of these lines, the only way we can approach them is as presented pictures which are suggested but somewhat vague to us, but which we must suppose are much clearer and more anguishing to Belinda. As readers we need the old-fashioned picture gallery theory of imagination to have any means of access to Belinda's mental life. This doesn't however, violate the 'impenetrable secrecy' of the imaging. We can guess, construe, and misconstrue, but there is no way we can see those images ("see" them) as Belinda does, since it is she who has a more or less faithful memory of them. We could read an encyclopedia article on eighteenth-century haircare, even see a demonstration or reconstruction of it, without feeling confident that we will ever be seeing as Belinda sees. Because feelings, as well as an academic interest in the proceedings, were part of the activity, as well as of the imaging of that activity. For us only the academic interest is pertinent.

The second set of lines has a different emphasis in terms of imaging, as one can see from the type of verbs used. In the earlier lines, the verbs all refer to the imagined activities themselves: binding the locks in paper-durance, straining the head with fillets, etc. Belinda presumably sees herself doing the binding and straining, which gives rise to the now-suspect theory of a series of pictures, each with its own governing verb. The combination of imagining the activities, and imagining

oneself doing the activities, makes this a complex case. The
second series of lines is clearer, in addition to upholding
Ryle's theory of imaging. "Methinks already I your Tears survey, / Already hear the horrid things they say." Not only has
the form of imaging changed here, but the tense has also changed.
Belinda is now anticipating, and partially because she has no
past images or precedents to work with, the emphasis has shifted
from the things "seen" or "felt," to the "seeing" and "hearing"
themselves. Belinda has no real images to see here, except
herself as "seeing" and "hearing." She is 'resembling a spec-
tator of her nursery,' as Ryle so neatly puts it.

Not only is this an affirmation of Ryle's theory, but it
is also an extremely subtle accomplishment for Pope. Pope is
presenting us with a picture of a woman picturing herself in the
position of "hearing" and "seeing" what imagined people might
someday be saying and thinking about her. Tracing the course
of this is almost too much for ordinary language, quite a bit
for poetic language, and even language analysis must pick itself up and fling itself at us in a breathless rush of shrewd
observations. It would be hard here, to say that either the
poetry or the language analysis were not worthy of the other,
weren't in some way mutually complementary. We sense the beginning of a new friendship.

C H A P T E R   I I I

GARCÍA MÁRQUEZ' LANGUAGE LABORATORY

i

Pope in general, and <u>The</u> <u>Rape</u> <u>of</u> <u>the</u> <u>Lock</u> in particular,
are a very special taste. They come from a world of miniatures,
intricate intaglios, announcements of doom on embroidered doi-
lies. Pope magnifies the small, telescopes the large, until his
art has that seductive air of homogeneity which is skill, and
not chance. The form in which Pope is writing--mock epic and
in heroic couplets--can only abet his distinctive style, because
it is a form that is finite, sketches a picture in one line and
concludes it in the next. As with most poetry, this form provides a palette that is restricted but intense, seared with the
colors of an existence which is small-scale but pointing the
way out of the perfume bottle and into the throne room. Language analysis has helped us see some of the painterly brushwork of a writer like Pope, and some of the ways that brushwork
could be extended to landscapes, moral statements, portraits of
queens. We were helped in our application of some of these
logico-analytical concerns by Pope's poetry being what it is.
By that we mean the demand that this poetry makes on itself
to say what it wants to in a very compact compass. So almost
any microtomic slice we take from the poem with the idea of
putting it under an electron microscope is certain to be suggestive and packed with linguistic information.

But in this chapter we intend to apply language analysis
to the form of literature most distant from poetry--the novel.
It is almost axiomatic that while poetry concentrates, the novel
elaborates. The novel is physically a much longer and more
diffuse type of writing than almost any other, and it permits
itself the privilege of an unhurried drawing away of the veil
of Maya. Since the whole of life isn't always caught in every
raindrop (one might say this is rarely the case), the novel
with its slow unfolding, introduction of characters that mimes
the way one would meet them in life, and various other "realistic" techniques, assumes its somewhat audacious place as a draw-
er together of life and art.

This is all very well for the novel, but for the language
analysts it poses a new sort of problem: Are we to regard the
novel with the same good-natured tolerance we accorded a poem
that stayed within artistic limits, or is it to be judged in
harsher terms, measured to see how closely it approaches the
reality it is miming? This latter requirement seems unnecessarily severe and perhaps even impossible, since one would have to
have a code or a series of formulae for translating statements
made within the novel into statements about the external world.
This conversion would have to have taken place before we could
ask ourselves what the statements "told us" about the world,
because the novel itself is not a source of primary information,
even though it may be overburdened with psychological insights
of various kinds, or with characters that seem particularly
"realistic."

Not only do novels talk about the external world, but
they also make use of it as an implicit model. (We are not
literal minded enough to push a view of the world as organized
into chapters, or as following any other such purely literary
convention. But we are speaking of temporal processes of growth

and change, dialogue that imitates human speech, the absence
for the most part of rhyme and meter, a narrator that takes the
place of eyes, etc. The list is endless.) Even atypical novels
like _Tristram Shandy_, which present experience in slow motion,
or stripped-down novels of the "nouveau roman" type, have life
as their standard. They are simply experimenting with new ways
of perceiving or describing life, some of which may be paradox-
ically closer to our actual experience of existence (which lacks
elaborate situating in a setting, or orderly presentation of
characters). But since a novel, although modelled on life, goes
on to tell its own story, it seems over-ambitious to expect
language analysis to tell us just how closely a particular novel
approaches life. Because one of the awarenesses the logical
positivists have tried to implant in us is the great number of
fallacious or meaningless statements that we make in our daily
transactions. Speaking accurately in a novel while still following the model becomes in these terms a highly problematic
undertaking, a Scylla and Charybdis joyride one would hesitate
to embark on. The only sane course therefore, seems to be that
of dealing with the novel on its own terms, looking at it as an
artistic creation within life, but not in any particular relation to it. Playing both sides against the middle, we will
permit ourselves allusions to external reality where they seem
inescapable. But no genre presuppositions will be made.

ii

It is fortunate for us that we have chosen to adopt this
position, because the novel we will consider in this chapter
poses a problem for categorizers. _Cien años de soledad_ by
Gabriel García Márquez, shares with a number of other Latin-
American novels the attribution, "realismo-mágico," or magic
realism. This sub-genre includes novels which possess the

shared characteristics of being realistic in structure but with
an overlay of fantasy which takes them completely out of Zola's
school of novel writing. They are a Latin-American specialty,
an escape hatch that masks criticism of dictatorship, as well
as a flexible combination that has all the advantages and disadvantages of shared worlds.

Those who have employed this technique have had various
degrees of success. A book like Mulata de tal by Asturias,
for example, seems not able to strike a balance between magic
and realism, with a resultant disorientation on the part of
the reader. Maybe this feeling of disorientation says something
about our expectations for novels. From a combination of habit,
literary convention, and something more intangible we'll call
"the demands of form," we feel when reading a novel that we
ought to be told a story, and that this story ought to have certain concrete touchdown points throughout. The story can be
fantastic, but certain orderly processes (like character development, for example) should be occurring in a sequential or semi-
sequential way, in order for us to feel intuitively that what
we are reading could legitimately replace certain experiences
we are not likely to have in life.

Cien años de soledad is crammed with such unlikely experiences, but done in such a way that we feel secure enough to
continue reading it, keeping one foot on the ground. The suggestive beginning of the novel is a good illustration of this:
"Muchos años después, frente al pelotón de fusilamiento, el
coronel Aureliano Buendía había de recordar aquella tarde remota
en que su padre le llevó a conocer el hielo."[18] This beginning

---

[18]Gabriel García Márquez, Cien años de soledad, (Buenos
Aires 1969) p. 9 (All subsequent García Márquez citations from
the same source.)

does a number of things, some of which fall to the province of
language analysis as we have interpreted it in the earlier chapters. Above all, the first sentence is a situating technique
that provides a temporal perspective which is somewhat convo-
luted. 'Years later in front of the firing squad' gives us
the sense of experience which is played out against a panorama
of memory, together with the feeling that everything to come
in the novel has already happened. The narrator then goes on
to talk about Macondo, the village that is the setting for the
novel, as it was in its early days, when Aureliano Buendía was
a child. So in substance we have a character who many years
later, and in an in extremis situation, is recalling his early
days, which coincide with the origin of Macondo. As a realistic device, this insertion of the description of Macondo into
the memory of Aureliano is convincing, because it makes the
events seem truer if they can be remembered. We alluded to the
role of the narrator in the preceding chapter, and this sort of
seeing through the eyes of a character, or a narrator (as Nick
Carraway in The Great Gatsby), seems one argument in favor of
the mediated telling of a story. Memory, to the language analysts, in no way guarantees the veracity of an account, which
may run the risk of being vitiated by subjective or faulty memory work that distorts the truth of occurrences.

But the idea that we do in fact represent things to ourselves, in the form of factual representations or object representations, is not to be dismissed as idle psychologizing.
That is what is happening here. The factual representation
Aureliano carries in his retinas, that of the firing squad aim-
ing its rifles at him, differs completely from the object representation in his mind, the day his father took him to discover
ice. The two representations do not fit together very well,
but they are nevertheless coexistent, showing the difficulty

with epistemological theories which impute a unilinear relationship between an object and the subject who appears to be thinking about that object. But the reader who is encompassing both
subject and object with his thought has to wait one hundred and
six pages for the filling out of the details of Aureliano's
object representation. It is not until then that the story
which begins in Aureliano's memory reaches the point at which
Aureliano is in fact in front of that same firing squad:

> Cuando el pelotón lo apuntó, la rabia se había
> materializado en una sustancia viscosa y amarga
> que le adormeció la lengua y lo obligó a cerrar
> los ojos. Entonces desapareció el resplandor de
> aluminio del amanecer, y volvió a verse a sí
> mismo, muy niño, con pantalones cortos y un lazo
> en el cuello, y vio a su padre en una tarde
> espléndida conduciéndolo al interior de la carpa,
> y vio el hielo. (p. 115)

Not only is this passage an amplification of Aureliano's
object representation, but it is also a form of private language,
as are all object representations that have a specific meaning
for particular individuals. (This is unlike the above-mentioned
geometry diagrams, which, though object representations, have
a meaning conferred by convention which is known to many.) What
Aureliano is thinking here is not known to the firing squad,
and is still only known fragmentarily to the reader who happened
to open the book to this page and read this description. We
know that he saw himself as a child in short pants, and that he
saw the ice, but beyond that we know nothing. What was the
ice like and what was his response to it? What anyway, is so
remarkable about ice? We reserve the last question until later,
but in order to answer the first two, we have to present yet one
more passage, which will complete the various perspectives of
Aureliano's object representation (although perspectives are,
even in pragmatic terms, almost inexhaustible).

Before we do though, we want to advance the tentative assertion that it is only in the novel as a genre that such a complete presentation of object representations is possible. This
seems to be a genre distinction, because for one thing, having
enough space for the leisurely exhibition of an object representation (call it image if you like) is important. For another,
a narrator who is omniscient helps get those images out of the
minds and before the reader. For a third, prose is often useful in making a private image comprehensible to the reader who
does not share this image (cf. the comparative lack of picture
Pope's 'earthly lover' leaves in our minds--with due apologies
to Ryle.) On the other hand, it is harder to stay on the track
of an image that unwinds itself over hundreds of pages, in the
form of foreshadowings, memory sequences, or other types of
temporal displacements. Unlike the earlier ones, today's novels
presuppose trained readers who aren't expecting (but are still
hoping for) a simple story. This emphasis placed on the telling of the story, rather than on the story itself, pushes the
contemporary novel in the general direction of a lyric poem.
From the point of view of language analysis therefore, today's
novel runs a somewhat smaller risk of being scrutinized as to
its closeness to reality. Self-conscious art forms don't present themselves as données.

Let's now look at the substance of Aureliano's object
representation, a full view of which probably appeared in his
mind as he faced the firing squad:

> Tanto insistieron, que José Arcadio Buendía
> pagó los treinta reales y los condujo hasta
> el centro de la carpa, donde había un gigante
> . . . Al ser destapado por el gigante, el cofre
> dejó escapar un aliento glacial. Dentro sólo
> había un enorme bloque transparente, con
> infinitas agujas internas en las cuales se
> despedazaba en estrellas de colores la claridad

> del crepúsculo. Desconcertado, sabiendo que
> los niños esperaban una explicación inmediata,
> José Arcadio Buendía se atrevió a murmurar:
> -Es el diamante más grande del mundo.
> -No--corrigió el gitano--. Es hielo. . .
> Aureliano dio un paso hacia adelante, puso la
> mano y la retiró en el acto. "Está hirviendo",
> exclamó asustado. Pero su padre no le prestó
> atención. . . Pagó otros cinco reales, y con
> la mano puesta en el témpano, como expresando
> un testimonio sobre el texto sagrado, exclamó;
> -Este es el gran invento de nuestro tiempo.
> (pp. 22-23)

This then, is Aureliano's association while he is in front
of the firing squad, a strongly-etched childhood memory whose
ontology is shared with that of the present moment. Both the
discovery of ice and imminent death by firing squad are moments
of surprise and disbelief, thresholds of a new consciousness,
and the death of former incarnations. Both are therefore related, like different senses of the same denotation. But we'll
keep that distinction for a more revelatory passage.

What is also surprising is the attitude toward ice that
is expressed in the book. The relationship of the characters
toward ice belongs more properly under our next topic, but we
cannot avoid at least mentioning it here, striking as it must
appear to a reader. Ice, the thing, the concrete embodiment of
the word "hielo" in Spanish, was not known in the mythically
pristine village of Macondo. A number of other "commonplace"
things brought by the gypsies were also unknown, like magnets
and telescopes. But that, and more, can be explained by the
description of the world at the time of the story: "El mundo
era tan reciente, que muchas cosas carecían de nombre, y para
mencionarlas había que señalarlas con el dedo" (p. 9). This
pre-Adamic statement about the newness of the world accords
well with the general emphasis of the book--Macondo as a microcosmic world, peopled with characters who seem the "first" of

their kind, who beget others, and through them dominate the
world for a time, until a final cataclysm destroys everything.
But more specifically, the quotation "points to" the question
of naming.

iii

A major preoccupation of Cien años de soledad is naming,
which of course takes many forms, and is also a major preoccupation of linguists everywhere. The exact relationship between
a designation and the object designated is a source of infinite
debate, because it seems to call into question assumptions about
language that are among the most basic. The issues here are
really pragmatic, and not ideological ones, because their im-
port is social and communicative. When we are naming an object,
how can we be certain that present and future auditors will
know what we are talking about? Henri Lefebvre, in his book
Le langage et la société, discusses this problem of naming:

> Si l'on énonce 'ce mur est gris', la proposition
> désigne un certain gris. Or ce gris est unique.
> Le terme général, le concept "gris" ne lui
> convient pas. Il faudrait, pour le désigner,
> un nom propre, dit Russell. Ou bien il
> suffirait de le montrer du doigt; c'est un
> "index" (et non pas un signe) de sorte que la
> proposition peut s'exclure de la logique
> symbolique.[19]

We are interested in this passage because it mentions
the action of pointing at objects, the same concern expressed
in Cien años de soledad. But pointing is just a symptom of
the difficulty of both indicating something specific, and also
locating it within the framework of symbolic logic. It is
really the old problem of how to name a particular so it is

---

[19]Henri Lefebvre, Le langage et la société (Paris 1966)
p. 98.

comprehensible in a more general context, or even at another
time. Specifying this grey wall (as opposed to another grey
wall) is not the deathless prose we suppose it at the time.
Only an elaborate videotape, with a very careful accompanying
explanation, could possibly preserve the specific meaning of
this grey wall for more than a few minutes. The simple linguistic and accompanying gestural activity is not enough. So obviously, in a system like that of symbolic logic, which likes
to feel it can explain everything using a finite number of symbols, or indeed in any system, designations and designata need
some firmer connection than a chance or occasional aptness.

It is rare that a novel concerns itself with the problem
of naming, particularly the sort of naming that is on the level
of pointing. But the concern with pointing at things in order
to indicate them is very much in keeping here, with the "neo-
primitivism" that the novel maintains, even as it veers in the
direction of social evolution. One of the marks of the primitive, even among present-day tribes, is a heavy dependence on
pointing. Nikolaus Marr describes this general phenomenon
found in tribes lacking a language as we know it:

> Tatsächlich war der Urmensch, der keine
> artikulierte Lautsprache beherrscht, froh,
> wenn er irgendwie auf einen Gegenstand
> hinweisen oder ihn vorzeigen konnte, und
> dazu verfügte er über eine besonders diesem
> Behufe angepasstes Werkzeug, über die Hand,
> die den Menschen so sehr von der übrigen
> Tierwelt auszeichnet . . . Die Hand oder
> die Hände waren die Zunge des Menschen.
> Handbewegungen, Mienenspiel und in einigen
> Fällen überhaupt Körperbewegungen
> erschöpften die Mittel sprachlichen Schaffens.[20]

---

[20]Nikolas Marr, "Über die Entstehung der Sprache," in
Unter dem Banner des Marxismus, 3 (1926) pp. 587-588.

This seems to imply that pre-verbal language is able to
exploit the particular and the situational better than more
formalized languages. Concepts that don't have an immediate
bearing on the particular context are not expressed, and it is
doubtful that they are even thought of. In any case, a wholly
gestural language simplifies the problem of particularizing,
and that of naming too. If you want something (like manioc),
you point at it, you've named it. The simplicity of the method
puts language analysis to shame. If only we didn't have to write
a history of ourselves. . .

Having long passed the golden age of inarticulateness,
and entered the era of neurasthenia, we now engage in the highly
rarefied (and by primitive standards, unnatural) activity of
examining the way we use language, often forgetting in the process its largely pragmatic origins. We worry whether our language adequately represents the world, whether it has the same
meaning to more than one person, even whether different classes
of people use a different vocabulary, and whether such a vocabulary can be itemized. The unexamined word is no more.

iv

Novels like Cien años de soledad share these and other
self-conscious concerns. Aureliano's discovery of ice was one
such example. Realismo mágico at its best and most convincing,
takes the commonplace and makes it strange, shows us how to
reexamine the world in the light of these new perspectives.
José Arcadio Buendía's failure to recognize ice (which is after
all possible in a tropical country) has the effect of making us
question the automatic nature of language-object relations.
In a novel, such relations are usually presupposed and taken
for granted, one of realism's preconditions being language that
effaces itself in pure functionalism. But once language begins

to be examined within a literary work itself, the displacement
of sense and emphasis is irrecoverable. A classic example of
this shift occurs in Sartre's La nausée, in the celebrated
scene where Roquentin looks at the roots of the chestnut tree.
In the course of staring at them, Roquentin suddenly feels that
they are a ding an sich, and very different from the language
we all use to refer to them. It is a frightening moment.

   Cien años de soledad also has its twinges of anxiety on
the score of language's not fitting quite perfectly the reality
it is related to. But here the source of unrest concerns
memory. It seems that the plague of insomnia which is making
the rounds of the world, has finally reached Macondo. The two
Indians who work for the Buendía family recognize the unmistak-
able signs of it. The disease is a strange one, because although
it prevents sleep, it leaves the victim feeling quite rested
and functional. So what is the problem, ask both the reader
and José Arcadio Buendía. The problem is, quite simply, that
after a prolonged period of insomnia, one day runs into the
next, and the sufferer starts to lose his memory. The practical
problem this causes, (and its relation to language analysis),
is shown in the following passage:

> Fue Aureliano quien concibió la fórmula que
> había de defenderlos durante varios meses de
> las evasiones de la memoria . . . Con un hisopo
> entintado marcó cada cosa con su nombre: mesa,
> silla, reloj, puerta, pared, cama, cacerola:
> Fue al corral y marcó los animales y las plantas:
> vaca, chivo, puerco, gallina, yuca, malanga,
> guineo. Poco a poco, estudiando las infinitas
> posibilidades del olvido, se dio cuenta de que
> podía llegar un día en que se reconocieran las
> cosas por sus inscripciones, pero no se recordara
> su utilidad. Entonces fue más explícito. El
> letrero que colgó en la cerviz de la vaca era
> una muestra ejemplar de la forma en que los
> habitantes de Macondo estaban dispuestos a
> luchar contra el olvido: Esta es la vaca,

> hay que ordeñarla todas las mañanas para que
> produzca leche y a la leche hay que hervirla
> para mezclarla con el café y hacer café con
> leche. Así continuaron viviendo en una
> realidad escurridiza, momentáneamente capturada
> por las palabras, pero que había de fugarse
> sin remedio cuando olvidaran los valores de la
> letra escrita. (p. 47)

This passage is certainly tailored to any number of language concerns, among them the question of sense and denotation
we discussed in the earlier chapters. Unusual conditions like
memory loss (or aphasia, which is being studied for what it can
tell us about normal speech acquisition and development), permit us to observe language's functioning at close range, as though
in slow motion. The novel's lucid account of the problems memory
loss poses is a case in point. Here, the writing of a word,
the assigning of a name, takes the place of the kind of connection which is normally made unconsciously, once the age of speech
learning is past. But when memory loss interferes with the
normal working out of this process, the assignment of names
becomes even more painfully arbitrary than it ordinarily is.
To put this in other terms, the relationship between sense and
denotation is no longer meaningful. The object (the animal
"cow," for example,) remains the same of course, but pointing
at it, denoting it in the old way is impossible. We now have
only a one-sided relationship, with the thing denoted, but
nothing that does the denoting. And since the sense (or senses)
of the denoted thing can only be defined in terms of the firm-
ness of the denotational relationship, then the sense, too,
has to change. In fact, without a clear denotation, any sense
is possible. Any way of describing an unspecified object is
valid. The wheel spins but moves nothing.

In the passage from Cien años de soledad, there seems to
be a very conscious effort to keep language functioning in the

old way, to keep it denoting, informing, specifying. And to
a certain extent they succeed. Life continues, the cow gets
milked, café con leche is consumed as in the old days. Then
what is the problem? What has changed? Fortunately for the
people of Macondo, the problem is of the sort that would only
concern a language analyst, and a very persnickety one at that.
In effect, this way of naming a cow "vaca," a chair, "silla,"
a pig, "puerco," is not really naming at all, as it would be
under other circumstances. It is rather describing.

In order to explain what we mean by calling this describing, we will refer to Bertrand Russell, one of the original
distinction-forming troublemakers. Russell has for some unknown
reason cathected on Sir Walter Scott, as many of Russell's examples concern him. In this case we have Sir Walter right where
we want him:

> . . . if 'Scott is Sir Walter' really means
> "the person named 'Scott' is the person named
> 'Sir Walter,'" then the names are being used
> as descriptions: i.e. the individual, instead
> of being named, is being described as the per-
> son having that name. This is a way in which
> names are frequently used in practice, and
> there will, as a rule, be nothing in the
> phraseology to show whether they are being used
> in this way or as names. When a name is used
> directly, merely to indicate what we are speak-
> ing about, it is no part of the fact asserted,
> or of the falsehood if our assertion happens
> to be false: it is merely part of the symbolism
> by which we express our thoughts . . . On the
> other hand, when we make a proposition about
> "the person called 'Scott,'" the actual name
> "Scott" enters into what we are asserting, and
> not merely into the language used in making
> the assertion. Our proposition will now be
> a different one if we substitute "the person
> called 'Sir Walter.'"[21]

---

[21]Bertrand Russell, Introduction to Mathematical Philosophy,
(London 1919), pp. 174-175.

This is a rather subtle point that Russell is making,
but there seems nevertheless to be a genuine difference between
names and descriptions. Names are merely formulae; they don't
change anything and their use is completely arbitrary. They
are labels that make the process of "referring to" easier.
But any agreed-upon label will do. Descriptions, obviously,
have more influence on the way the globe turns. The manner in
which we describe an object in a proposition determines the
truth or falsity of that proposition. Descriptions enter into
active relationships with other linguistic elements. But almost any unjaundiced observer can notice name/description differences on that level. As Russell makes clear, it is where
the descriptions sound like names that the trouble starts.
Names and descriptions here resemble each other in a misleading
way, just as "do not kill," and "killing is evil" are really
the same, but appear different. Language analysts are fond of
clinging to this slippery area, where differences are not really
differences, and similarities lead us down a treacherous path.
But it is these linguistic acrobats that give jobs to the rest
of us netmen down below.

The point we want to make in this "memory-loss" passage,
is that what appear to be names, and what would be names in
normal language functioning, are really descriptions. "Vaca"
is not used arbitrarily here. Attaching the word "vaca" to the
cow, is a desperate attempt to keep the function of that noun
before our eyes, and especially, before the eyes of Macondo.
That the cow is called "vaca" does not matter, but that the
entity referred to as "vaca," has four legs and gives milk, is
what is really important in this label-pinning. So saying here,
"This is a cow," is not a way of naming that animal, but of
distinguishing it from say, a chair. We are therefore dealing

with descriptions, and not names, which is here the symptom of
a language breakdown due to memory loss.

v

Another concern of this passage is the difference between
the meaning of words and their use: "Poco a poco . . . se dio
cuenta de que podía llegar un día en que se reconocieran las
cosas por sus inscripciones, pero no se recordara su utilidad."
These lines suggest a special way of "meaning," that by which
we recognize things. Is recognition first of all the same thing
as meaning-furnishing? If we label an ocelot so as to recognize
it in a zoo which contains other felines, can we then automatically say we know what it means to be an ocelot? Isn't a case
in point of this distinction furnished by the more "modern"
road signs that eliminate written language altogether, and just
use pictures? Aren't there some in which we can recognize all
the objects pictured in the signs, yet not be sure what they
mean? (For example, a block picture of an automobile beneath
the tires of which are two s-curves--how do we know that this
means, caution! slippery when wet! and not, feel free to cut
up!) But are we in fact recognizing the picture, if we are not
sure about its meaning? Doesn't knowing the meaning have to
precede, or at least accompany, recognition?

What is recognition? Etymologically, it is a reknowing,
a knowing again. This implies that one has to have known something the first time in order to know it again, that recognition
demands some sort of pre-knowledge. In recognizing an object
then, I must be able to imagine what it is I am to recognize.
Perhaps "imagine" is too exigent--maybe I only need an idea of
the thing, maybe someone else's description of it. Maybe even
an object which is similar to it, but differs from it in a
describable particular, would do. Or a coherent series that is

lacking in just the one thing--our object. (Many intelligence tests are structured on just such a principle.) The possibilities seem endless, concerning the particular way one recognizes an object, but the common factor seems to be some aperture for pre-knowledge, having a prior idea with which to compare it. Does this then imply, that one has to know first what something means, in order to be able to recognize it? Probably the two can be collapsed into one. While recognition has that "pre" element, which "knowing the meaning" strictly speaking lacks, for all practical epistemological purposes, the two are the same, and produce the same results.

Accepting this identity, how do we then feel about the conjunction of recognizing an object with not remembering its use? Wittgenstein, in his Investigations, says that the meaning of a word is its use in language.[22] The García Márquez passage says something very different. These do, in fact, seem two opposing viewpoints concerning meaning in language, presupposing different functions. Language here is defined either as what it can do, or what it is in itself. Actually, this dichotomy is not precisely accurate, because any theory about language has as its base an attempt to explain what language is. Few succeed, of course, because all theories to date have been limited to the resources of language itself, while giving such explanations. There is something a little suspect about the whole process.

Some theorists, like Roman Jakobson, feel that a functional approach to language theory solves the "metalanguage" problem. They don't try to decide what language is, but rather what it does, by classifying statements into various categories, depending on the purpose of the statement. Thus, a statement having

---

[22]Ludwig Wittgenstein, Philosophical Investigations, (43).

an emotive function will differ in kind from one having an in-
formative function, etc. It is somewhat like what Carnap has
been telling us, except that he has jumped a little ahead of
Jakobson. While Jackobson is concerned with finding differences
in use, Carnap presupposes these differences, but shows how they
are often couched in the resemblance of form. Still, the orientation is similar in both cases.

Is functionalism perhaps the closest we can come to understanding what language is? This point of view certainly accounts
for much of what language does. Language communicates, expresses, influences, records phenomena, expresses amenities, frames
thoughts, and clearly does numerous other things which don't
at this instant leap to the mind of this author. All of these
are functions of language, even though in actuality they may not
be so clearly set off from one another as this list makes them
appear. So why not explain language in this manner, instead of
seeking some inexpressible way of describing what language really
is? We must admit that the idea is very attractive, permitting
us as it does to feel that we are making progress in language
encompassment at the same time as we are using language.

In Jakobson's theory there is even a slot for metalanguage,
called, appropriately enough, the "metalinguistic function."
The concept behind this function is rather simple. Metalanguage
occurs any time a person steps back from what he was saying in
order to comment on it. An example of this would be something
like the following: "You seem quite happy today. By happy I
mean you are smiling, your eyes are glowing, and you can't seem
to talk seriously for a second." For Jakobson then, metalanguage needn't be a profound or out of reach philosophical concept. It is rather something that often occurs in daily language use. Calling this sort of occurrence "metalanguage" is

a simple solution to the talking-about-language-with-language
problem. We haven't yet seen a better solution from the "what
is language" school.

So can we just go ahead and accept the idea that the meaning of language is its use? Then how do we reconcile this deci-
sion with the problem the novel poses, that of recognizing things
by their inscriptions, but not remembering their use? We concluded earlier that for practical purposes, recognition and
knowing the meaning are the same. The people of Macondo seem
to be saying that they know the meaning of language-objects,
while not remembering their use.

As always, there have to be a number of ways to explain
this. The one is, that in spite of Jakobson, knowing the meaning and knowing use are really two different things. Knowing
the meaning tells us something about the language-object, but
doesn't exhaust the possibilities for ontological situating.
So an additional area of knowledge, known as "use," must be
supplied for us to have a complete functional knowledge of the
object. (It seems possible to describe a chair down to minute
particulars, and yet not say it is for sitting. Unless of
course, one believes in the Platonic idea of a chair, in which
case its use would have to be given or understood in the very
naming.) Another point almost too obvious to mention, is that
Jakobson's system presupposes normal language functioning, not
memory loss, so that the use distinction is peculiar to this
case. The third point involves making a distinction between
words and objects. Perhaps the Macondo characters have not for-
gotten the use of words themselves, but of objects. They know
that the word "cow" refers to that animal, but whether or not
they know that the animal "cow" is used for giving milk, is
secondary.

The complexities to this distinction are considerable. Because on the one hand can be said that knowing the word cow (not the object) anyway presupposes the knowledge that the word cow is associated with milk-giving, as part of its definitional meaning. This view implies that one of the uses of the word "cow" is its embodiment in the object "cow." And the cow-object gives milk. The problem is even more excruciating for objects that don't have a use that is structured even to the extent that that of "cow" is. A stone, for example, has a potentially limitless range of uses, among them, as a missile for throwing, an ingredient in construction, a piece in a game, to name just a few. So can we really know what a stone is, if we sedulously avoid knowing its use? Certainly the various functions of stones will demand different ways of speaking about them. "The stones were crushed for concrete." "How would you like me to drop this stone on your head?" Not only is "stone" used in grammatically different ways in these two sentences, but it also has a completely different affective status. It would be pleasant, but inaccurate, to say that the grammatical or even syntactic structure reflects the affective difference and ultimately becomes a pattern for meaning. This correspondence is unfortunately not usually observable, except in phrases whose convention-conferred use is so strict that the particular grammatical form inevitably occurs whenever the phrase itself is used. And although more than one theory has been built on agreeable exceptions, such a revolutionary theory as grammar-dominated meaning could hardly sustain itself on such flimsy evidence. And we are not in fact speaking about grammar here, in its normative schoolroom sense, but about the use of words, possibly a subtle distinction, but only if we ignore the difference between the individual and the collective. By that I mean the difference between the use of "stone," and the use of nouns. It is the

enormous difference between knowing what to do to defend your-
self, and knowing the correct completion of a paradigm.

We began this discussion of the difference or identity
of meaning and use of words in a genuine spirit of indecision.
We had on the one hand Macondo's feeling that in progressive
amnesia it would recognize what a cow was, but not its use.
On the other hand we had before us Wittgenstein's dictum that
the meaning of a word is its use in language. In the course
of playing with the possibilities, using examples, we seem to
have veered toward Wittgenstein. In experiential terms at least,
the meaning of a word varies enormously with its particular use
on a given occasion. We've seen that, I think, with "stone,"
and the reader can repeat the experiment with a significantly
large number of words. Think, for example, of words that have
different meanings, depending on whether they are used concretely or abstractly. Or think of "shop talk," or common words
that have specific meanings in particular fields (like "bed" in
geology). Accurately identifying the use of a particular word
requires vigilance and a spirit that is willing to be a cataloguing one. The Oxford English Dictionary is a large demonstration of this approach, formidable enough to frighten the
neophyte, who is rarely even conscious of the evolutions in
word use that take place during his lifetime. Judging by the
discrepancies in language, and the genuinely haphazard way it
circumscribes objects, the use argument is a compelling and
realistic one. We can only hope, in the midst of all this,
that Macondo's cows will still be milked.

There is one final point we want to make about this passage, which has proven an excellent jumping-off point for theories about language. This last point involves, fittingly, the
last line of the passage: "Así continuaron viviendo en una
realidad escurridiza, momentáneamente capturada por las palabras

pero que había de fugarse sin remedio cuando olvidaran los valores de la letra escrita." The line suggests, in a final access of language-consciousness, that language is the means by which reality is "captured," and without it reality would slip away. This sounds like a surprisingly radical point of view, one which can only be satisfactorily explained by the battle against amnesia's incursions. Because somewhere in the implicit heart of most critics is the assumption that reality precedes and will survive the language that seeks to describe it. The debate usually centers around language's ability to represent or picture reality, and how pellucid a medium it is for this purpose. Or the fact that language conveys information about reality, but doesn't really picture it. Or other, similarly structured concerns. But all are posited with reference to reality which is the model and pattern for language.

In the final line of the passage, reality is ephemeral; its continued presence depends on its being captured by language. Not only language in general, but even more specifically written language, that of the signs attached to tables, herbs, and goats. It is a rather solipsistic approach to the world, the ship in the bottle marked "et nunc et semper." It is also the novel's (generically speaking) assertion of preeminence in a world of arbitrary realities, where nothing is ordered and everything is trouvé. The novel can, must, order its reality with language, the only tool it has. In a sense it is always pinning names on reality, but not usually in so direct a manner. Macondo itself is a distillation from the memory of its inhabitants, and the impressions of its readers. And for the duration of its artistic existence, it is a signpost, a language placecard picked from among many, one of the 'values of the written letter.' For the novel, there is no other reality.

The passage we just looked at is indisputably part of
the novel's story, showing the precise means of Macondo's battle against amnesia. But it is also, in its way, explicitly
about language and language functioning, describing, and at the
same time showing us what it describes, and how it describes.
But novels that make any claim for realism, or even seek to
tell a sequential story, can't always travel on their bellies
in this way. A substantial part of the novel must describe the
story directly, reserving language to comment on the events,
or the characters, but not on language. (An exception is the
kind of novel that creates a built-in structure for language
to comment on itself, like Gide's Faux-Monnayeurs. Here, the
device of having a journal to talk about the events and writing
of the novel, is quite effective, and facilitates dizzying shifts
of ontology.)

vi

To see better the range of Cien años de soledad, we'll
look at a passage which is purely descriptive, with no particularly self-conscious concerns. But in order for it to make any
sense, we first have to situate it a bit. The passage describes
Rebeca, who as an orphan girl finds her way to the Buendía family and stays with them for many years. Her main peculiarity
is her desire to eat earth, a habit which her new family breaks
her of only by the most drastic means. But her hunger for earth
is 'older than she,' and any emotional situation causes the need
to reappear. The passage we will consider involves just such
a situation. Rebeca is in love with an Italian music teacher,
Pietro Crespi, and so is her "sister" (the Buendía's daughter,
Amaranta). There is naturally fierce competition between the
two girls, which compounds the normal strain of loving. The
passage reflects this strain:

Se echaba puñados de tierra en los bolsillos,
y los comía a granitos sin ser vista, con un
confuso sentimiento de dicha y de rabia . . .
Los puñados de tierra hacían menos remoto y más
cierto el único hombre que merecía aquella
degradación, como si el suelo que él pisaba con
sus finas botas de charol en otro lugar del
mundo, le transmitiera a ella el peso y la
temperatura de su sangre en un sabor mineral que
dejaba un rescoldo áspero en la boca y un
sedimento de paz en el corazón.
                                (p. 61)

Much is going on in this passage, on various levels.
Rebeca is as of old, eating earth. But that "simple" pleasure
is no longer simple. It is a habit she has been trained to be
ashamed of, so she eats the earth with a complex mixture of feelings, not all of them wholly pleasurable. But in this passage,
eating earth is responding to a specific need, unlike the un-
differentiated need of childhood. However, this need is shown
to us through a very complicated metaphor, something the language analysts can very soon get their teeth in. The first part
of it is, 'The handfuls of earth made the only man who deserved
such degradation seem less remote and more certain.' A cause-
and-effect relationship is being set up between the eating of
earth and insuring the proximity and certainty of the chosen
man. In logical terms this is absurd, since Pietro Crespi has
no knowledge of the sacrifice that is being made for him. And
while clairvoyance and premonition are another illogical but
living part of the book, even that sort of "explanation" is not
the case here. The connection is only logical on the metaphorical level, where justifications are rarely of the cause-and-
effect sort, and much more usually purely linguistic and associational. The second part of that same sentence completes the
wide-ranging metaphor: 'as if the earth on which he walked
with his fine, patent leather boots in another area of the world

transmitted to her the weight and temperature of his blood in
a mineral taste that left a bitter ash in the mouth and a sediment of peace in the heart.' This multiple, gustatory metaphor
is surely as complicated as some of Donne's. Before we can
examine it from the point of view of language analysis, we first
have to decide what it is saying, and how it is working.

The first connection we can make is that between the handfuls of earth and the earth on which Pietro Crespi walks. This
is the element which unites them in Rebeca's mind. But the two
earths are very different. First of all, they are in widely
separated parts of the world. And secondly, the two earths are
treated very differently. The one is consumed, an activity which
forces the eater into a very intimate knowledge of every grain,
every worm and insect that resides in that handful of earth.
The other is trodden upon depreciatingly, in sense-isolating
patent leather boots, that lack even the porousness of leather.
Yet the image of earth, everywhere and under everything, unites
these two very different beings and activities. Not only is it
a common element in their activities, but it is also a medium
of metaphorical transmission. She can feel the weight and temperature of his blood with every mouthful she eats, because
she can (figuratively) taste his blood, by eating the same thing
he walks on. The complexities grow as we follow each successive
step of this metaphor. To Rebeca, the blood has a mineral taste
(which is also presumably, that of the earth--the scientific
spirit has not succeeded in causing me to verify this). This
taste does two things to Rebeca: 1) It leaves a bitter ash in
her mouth, and 2) It leaves a sediment of peace in her heart.
Whether it is the taste of the earth which leaves these things,
or the taste of the blood, or both, is unclear.

Language analysis would look askance at this passage.
We have already commented on the logical absurdity of Rebeca's

eating earth in order to make Crespi seem closer. No amount of earth consumed by Rebeca could ever make these discrete states or activities a part of one another, except in the disallowed psychological realm, which has its own laws. The second part of the passage is guilty of a category mistake (or perhaps, several category mistakes, depending on how particular one wants to be). The trouble all starts with the hypothetical "as if," which, syntactically, is an indicator that what will follow is not the case, but is a sort of wish-fulfillment, a desire that circumstances be different from what they are in fact. "As if" statements are dangerous, because persons who go to the trouble of formulating them usually have something very particular and detailed to say in them. The well-documented private dream. The reader or auditor often loses sight of the hypothetical nature of the statement uttered, by the time all its outlines have been lovingly traced out. Here, the "as if" leads to the earth's transmission to Rebeca of the weight and temperature of Crespi's blood. Even if Crespi were two feet away, instead of in another part of the world, such a transmission could never take place. It violates basic laws of physics. The shock waves from his tread could conceivably be transmitted to her, although not precisely from her eating the earth, but never the quality of his blood. So we have a category mistake which involves the incompatibility of a _percipi_ and the means by which it has become that _percipi_, a physical and perceptual problem.

But the trouble doesn't end there. Accepting for the sake of simplicity that blood weight and temperature can actually be transmitted, we find that this transmission has occurred by means of a "mineral taste," which is not strictly that of blood or that of earth. The distance from Crespi's walking on the earth to Rebeca's having a mineral taste of his blood, is very great. And so many obstacles involving the nature of liquids

and solids and their possible transmutations have to be over-
come, that "category mistake" is almost too weak a charge to
level. Short of "nonsense" which we don't want to utter here
and throw up our hands, "category mistake" is the most appropriate term from the language analysts' arsenal.

But what follows is even more unclear, in terms of categories. Because this is a mineral taste 'that left a bitter
ash in her mouth and a sediment of peace in her heart.' The
categories are really hopelessly mixed, by this point in the
sentence. Now an intangible like "taste," is leaving palpable
consequences, like ashes and sediments. The grammatical structure that puts the ash and the sediment in a dependent clause
governed by "mineral taste," makes the relationship syntactically
unambiguous, although it is logically impossible, since it presupposes that concrete and abstract entities[23] are able to function in the same ways. The verb "leave," with its object, ac-
complishes a linguistic transition which is unsupportable, again
with reference to logical laws like those of cause-and-effect,
or even to elementary scientific laws, like the fact that ashes
only result from complete combustion of materials.

Continuing with this line of concrete/abstract category
mistake, we find it surprising that Rebeca should have a bitter
ash in her mouth from eating earth. We can be less literal-minded
and say that bitter here is used metaphorically and refers to
an emotional state, but that probably only makes things worse.
Because now we're mixing concrete nouns and abstract modifying

---

[23]"Abstract entity" is a concept that has been under much
discussion by certain language analysts, who believe it is a
contradiction in terms to juxtapose these two words. We are
not taking sides by using them, merely seeking a convenient
formula for pointing to the problem here.

adjectives. The illogical relationship is more intimately and inextricably interwoven. But "bitter ash" may still conceivably refer to the actual taste of the ash, and thereby enter into its physical description in an entirely normal way. (Ashes are grey, they crumble when touched, they taste bitter, etc.) But no such excuse can be invoked for 'sediment of peace.' That is the purest of category mistakes, the assignment of an abstract quality to the most concrete of substances, a sediment. No amount of rationalization can save this phrase from condemnation. Although, ironically, "sediment" is the first noun we've heard in a long time that carries attention back to the beginning of the sentence, where Rebeca is eating the earth. So "sediment" has logical antecedents, but they are vitiated by the attachment to it of the word "peace," not only suspect in this combination, but having in itself the undefinable quality of words like 'good' and 'beauty.'

Obviously, the entire sentence in its intricate juxtapositions, has violated not only the laws of logic, but even those of conversational speech. What can we say in García Márquez' defense? Well, on the level of realism, we can say that the sentence either mimes the tortuous route of Rebeca's agonized thought, or the journey of the earth along her alimentary canal. Either would explain the frequent shifts, the transformation of one material into another, as the mind converts thoughts into other thoughts in its constant efforts at solutions, or as the digestive apparatus goes through its well-known process of breaking down solid materials. Viewed in these terms, the sentence carries a very sensuous image, so sensuous that it doesn't quite fit the contours of human speech, which is the form it must of course take.

So we have the ever-lamented paradox of the poverty of
the language through which the world is represented, which is
anyhow the only way the world <u>can</u> be represented (as opposed
to the world's <u>presenting itself</u>, or the world as a given,
either of which we are forced to handle in its undigested form,
to borrow from our burgeoning metaphor). But this is the kind
of paradox one becomes desperately embroiled in only if one is
bent on seeing language as picturing reality, which we have
agreed is not practical.

It would be more accurate, although less dramatic, to
say that language pictures or displays its own syntax, which
governs its presentation of itself. That is why we have the
feeling of discomfort that we do, while reading sentences like
that about Rebeca's eating earth. There is nothing wrong with
the grammar, precisely. It is something more intangible, but
nonetheless felt, the sort of deep structure that lends author-
ity to certain clauses, which usually govern and shape the
form of succeeding clauses or phrases. In the repeated transformations and permutations of even the sense of certain phrases
in our example, something went wrong with the syntactic hierarchy.
And that something is more insidious than simply an ungrammatical
sentence, which is easily diagnosed and corrected. Because there
is nothing technically wrong with this sentence on the structural level, just that the syntactical connections presuppose
a logical concatenation of materials, which we have seen is not
always the case.

Apparently, this feeling of 'syntactic discomfort' has
its origins in biological and therefore inter-linguistic considerations. E. H. Lenneberg, in "A Biological Perspective of
Language," tells us,

> Although language families are so different,
> one from the other, that we cannot find any
> historical connexion between them, every lan-
> guage, without exception, is based on the same
> <u>universal</u> <u>principles</u> of semantics, syntax, and
> phonology. All languages have words for rela-
> tions, objects, feelings, and qualities, and
> the semantic differences between these denotata
> are minimal from a biological point of view
> . . . Language universals are the more remark-
> able as the speakers live in vastly different
> types of cultures ranging from an essentially
> neolithic type to the highly complex cultural
> systems of Western civilization. Further,
> language and its complexity is independent of
> racial variation. It is an axiom in linguis-
> tics that any human being can learn any lan-
> guage in the world. Thus, even though there
> are differences in physical structure, the
> basic skills for the acquisition of language
> are as universal as bipedal gait.[24]

The universality of these linguistic relations extends the
range of our self-justifying possibilities. Linguists can tell
us precisely why a certain sentence might sound "wrong" to us,
by comparing the sentence with universal semantic schemes.
But what filters down to the layman appears to take the form
of a "convention," a formula that is hallowed by long, unconscious use.

Without certain syntactical conventions, of course, we
would hardly be able to point to the source of our discomfort
when reading the sentence. To say that it is guilty of certain
category mistakes is to employ a formula which is useful as a
pointer in the direction of the problem. But an even larger
sense of the pathology of this sentence is needed here, because

---

[24]E. H. Lenneberg, "A Biological Perspective of Language,"
in <u>Language</u>, ed. R. C. Oldfield & J. C. Marshall (Middlesex
1968), pp. 33-34.

the connections it is making are sublinguistic, the product of
a diseased psyche, which Rebeca's undoubtedly is. Her need to
eat earth, to feel in it certain atavistic sensations which she
views as somehow linking her with a man she loves much too
fiercely, can all be felt or intuited in the chaotic yet desperately controlled structure of this sentence, which doesn't
exceed the limits of grammar, yet doesn't live up to the expectations of logic, either. García Márquez has done well here,
to violate logical rules a little, to commit flamboyant category mistakes. Because the logical laws presuppose sane and
orderly language uses, and reflecting Rebeca's peculiarities is
certainly not one of them. She is best lured and captured by
the kind of language that follows her underground and then comes
up the other side, entwining itself with the stones and the mag-
gots, passing easily from one density of signification to another. That sort of language puts too much pressure on paradigms.

viii

There are certain metaphors in the novel which don't always help the sense along. They on the contrary fulfill the
gloomiest predictions of the logical positivists, destroying
sense in the process of breaking down categories. Our example
of this involves a dialogue, so not only is our own comprehension at stake, but that of the characters as well:

> Aureliano comprobó [que estaban solos], antes
> de levantar la vista y encontrarse con los ojos
> de Pilar Ternera, cuyo pensamiento era
> perfectamente visible, como expuesto a la luz
> del mediodía.
>   -Bueno -dijo Aureliano-. Dígame qué es.
>   Pilar Ternera se mordió los labios con una
> sonrisa triste.

> -Que eres bueno para la guerra -dijo-. Donde
> pones el ojo pones el plomo.
> Aureliano descansó con la comprobación del
> presagio. Volvió a concentrarse en su trabajo,
> como si nada hubiera pasado, y su voz adquirió
> una reposada firmeza.
> -Lo reconozco -dijo-. Llevará mi nombre.
> (p. 72)

Even without having read the rest of the novel, one can see from
the passage that there is a certain psychic link between
Aureliano and Pilar Ternera. After all, "her thought was perfectly visible, as though exposed to the midday light." If we
have read other parts of the book, we know that Pilar Ternera is
a fortune teller whose predictions are usually accurate, and that
Aureliano often has surprising premonitions. In another vein,
we would also know that Aureliano and Pilar Ternera have had in-
tercourse of a non-spiritual nature as well. So all of this explains the possibility of cryptic speech between these two characters. But although their thought may be very open, the one to
the other, the reader doesn't have the privilege of this kind
of easy accessibility. So a metaphor like 'eres bueno para la
guerra. Donde pones el ojo pones el plomo,' comes as a complete
shock to the reader, who up until this point was following the
dialogue with confidence. Because on the surface, 'where you
put your eye you put your bullet' seems like a very simple,
descriptive statement, testifying to accuracy of marksmanship.
In any case it doesn't sound like a particularly dramatic thing
to say about a person. But Pilar Ternera seems unusually convulsed
before she utters it. And we know that logically, a simple statement about Aureliano's abilities would not be the occasion of
so much emotion. So what can be the meaning of this phrase,
which doesn't any longer seem to have anything to do with tar-
get practice?

It is only when Aureliano answers that we begin to understand: 'I recognize him' he says, 'He will bear my name.' We are finally told--and even now not explicitly--what Pilar Ternera is talking about. She is going to have a child whose father is Aureliano. Simply that. But in this case the metaphor comes from a completely different field of human experience (not taking into consideration here the famous love and war juxtaposition, or the equation of lovemaking and aggression by certain contemporary feminist writers).

In the passage about eating earth, the metaphor was circuitous and even synaesthetic, so one wouldn't want to say naively that that metaphor, as opposed to this one, was 'plain to the senses or intellect.' Yet its form seemed somehow the right way to talk about a character like Rebeca, in any place other than a clinical report. The reader puts up with, and even welcomes the convolutions of sense, feeling himself on the road to a more complete, intuitive understanding of Rebeca and her sensuous world. While Pilar Ternera's metaphor comes as an unsettling (though temporary) obfuscation of sense. Because the situation she is describing has none of the biological complexity of that of Rebeca. So it doesn't demand a metaphor which testifies by its form to a factitious complexity of thought.

Perhaps the reader's indignation at bumping into a phrase which leaves him confused, points to his feeling that something private is occurring, from which he has been excluded in advance. It is not surprising that two characters who live largely cerebral and interior lives should understand each other better than we, as readers, understand them. The fact that they can utter such phrases and be understood shows that their existence is carried on in a realm that is governed by laws other than those of ordinary discourse. Theirs is a psychic and

psychological language, which may avail itself of the syntax
of everyday speech, (thereby disqualifying it, for Wittgenstein,
from being an absolutely private language) but in which words
are symbols or emblems of things other than their apparent meaning, displaced denotations, as it were.

ix

In the first chapter, we spoke about the psychological
symbolism potentially inherent in emotive statements, which is
one of the reasons they assume non-logical forms. Because unlike, 'the table is red, small, and in the corner of the room,'
symbolic utterances don't point in such a straight line to any
object. Symbols, Jungian archetypes, and other grandiose, conceptual affirmations of this ilk, have long lost their moment
in the sun. Critical theories whose support systems are largely
centered in such shadowy areas have only limited appeal, and
that almost exclusively to frustrated Utopians seeking a way to
construe things as other than they are, or highschool English
majors. Nevertheless, we see symbolism functioning in small
ways on a daily basis (in the means of transportation individuals
choose, in their food preferences or the color they paint their
kitchens, the name they assign to their dogs, or the things they
say when they are not fully awake).

Even as smooth a character as Lefebvre, in the midst of
talk about the latest structuralist theories, feels an unac-
countable urge once again to put the spector of symbolism to
rest, with new adjectives to line its coffin. Let's hear what
he says about it:

> Considerons maintenant le symbole. La
> confusion s'aggrave. Les uns tirent le
> symbole du côté de l'expressif, du spontané,
> de l'affectif. Pour les psychanalystes, les

symboles émergent de l'abyssal. Le bois, la
pierre, le bâton, le trou, la ferre, le ciel,
de multiples objets, symbolisent, dans les
rêves comme dans le langage, le père ou la
mère. Impossible de parler sans faire appel
à ces brusques surcharges affectives qui
pèsent sur certains mots, parce qu'elles se
joignent étroitement à certains choses. Le
symbole est à la fois cause et raison; il
agit sans méditation, directement; il produit
les blocages de l'intellect, de la conscience,
de la raison raisonnante. Au-delà d'un seuil
mal déterminé, ou en deça, le symbolisme devient
morbide, soit que la censure l'interdise et
coupe le circuit de la communication, soit que
l'effort pour transmettre le symbole devienne
epuisant.[25]

This sounds like a good two-minute summary of the role of symbolism through the ages. The dispute as to whether symbols
come from an area of innocent affectivity, or suggest by their
very nature something much more sinister, will never be put
definitely to rest. What is more interesting is what Lefebvre
says the symbol in itself is 'at once cause and reason, acting
without mediation, and a blockage of thought.' Viewed in this
way, symbolic language doesn't need to give an account of itself. It just _is_ the way objects themselves are. Such an extreme laissez-faire attitude if applied universally, would be
the death of language analysis. Because almost every word
would be correct in existing, simply because it exists. This
would be fine for a philosophical system based entirely on
tautologies, which by their very nature are always true, but
for any other system, this non-critical attitude would be fatal.

So we obviously can't adopt symbolism as a battle cry,
and shout it in the midst of every linguistic difficulty. But
there are certain times when doing literature (or whatever)

---

[25]Lefebvre, op. cit., pp. 112-113.

justice demands interpreting it symbolically. Such a time was
the passage where Rebeca ate earth, and such a time, also, was
the confrontation between Aureliano and Pilar Ternera. Rebeca's
earth-eating in classical symbolic terms, is her search for the
mother she never knew; her need for an advising mother figure
is heightened by her semi-hysterical amorous state, so she eats
earth and through this action puts herself in touch with ancient
and continuous rhythms and forces. Since the earth is not
really a mother, but only stands for or symbolizes a mother,
this explains the synaesthesia of the passage, so alien to rigorous language analysis. Because one sense stands for another,
in a direct relation to the way earth stands for mother. So
for example, the pleasure of eating earth and imbibing the pri-
mordial minerals, may well be related to the pleasure a baby
gets from nursing, an activity whose continuum in memory was
broken by the loss of Rebeca's parents (here, mother) whose
presence she constantly strives to recreate and simulate.

When symbols are viewed as being sufficient and exact in
themselves, there is virtually no distance between a symbol
and the thing it symbolizes. If earth is understood and accepted as a symbol for mother, one doesn't try to line up all
the physical similarities of the two objects, or of the object
and its concept. The relationship once established (and there
is admittedly some logical reason for juxtaposing the two),
there is no further need for rationalization of this relationship. As Lefebvre says, symbols facilitate thought blockages,
and this is precisely the way they do it. But pragmatically,
the earth isn't really a very satisfying substitute for mom.
It will never replace that bustling little woman, that large,
indolent woman, that silent, scowling woman, that indulgent,
oversimplifying woman, we all have somewhere in our neurotic
past. A symbol will never carry the groceries in, pave the

driveway, or really take the place of what it is symbolizing. And the same is true for Rebeca. Her actual distance from her lost mother is very great, and will never be fully bridged by even the largest imaginable quantity of consumed earth. That is why although they undoubtedly have merit in psychological terms, and furnish us with convenient shorthand notation, symbols of this sort don't really help us when we go to look for logical relations among objects, and between language and its objects.

But we felt a need here to go through a kind of exercise in symbolism, doing what critics do when they feel they know in advance all there is to be said about a work, or a portion thereof. In this way we took the relation, earth=mother, because one of the classical abstract qualities of earth has long been its motherlike nature, as the source of nourishment for so many living things. That is our justification for setting up such an equation initially, and once we set it up, it is relatively easy to fill in all the contributing details. This sort of critical activity is much like a puzzle, where finding the single key permits the happy falling into place of all the corresponding parts.

At this point we have argued ourselves into the position of being undecided as to whether symbolism is an aid or an impediment to logic. On the aid side, we can first of all point to the wide use of symbolic notation by structuralists and people who work with symbolic logic. This, in itself, is not a justification of symbolism's place in logic, because symbols conceived in this way are more nearly low-level technical facilitations than facilitations of method, just as having written symbols for words facilitates the widespread transmission of thought, but doesn't in any way constitute that thought. We still haven't shown that symbolism is an aid to logic in any substantive way. What about in our example? It seems clear that the apparent discrepancies in logic disappear (or are at least diminished) by the acceptance of a symbolic interpretation for the passage. In effect we have a symbolic substructure, which has its own logic of organization, which may not appear to be logic on a more superficial level of organization. (As we alluded to earlier, this explanation is a little like Chomsky's conception of "deep structures," which reflect the actual, and not always apparent, equivalences among different languages. But we are over-simplifying wildly on all fronts.)

This then, is more or less our argument for symbolism as the handmaiden of logic. We are also quite willing to see symbolism as one of logic's impediments. On the most literal level, what isn't on the page doesn't exist. The logical positivists want to see things in writing, and in the flesh. Beyond that is metaphysics. So what right have we to imagine a subversive deeper level, a catch-all for everything that doesn't make sense on the visible level? In addition, if symbolism, even in individual cases, really furnishes us with a complete detail by detail picture, almost a worldview, how can we feel as though an external logic can have any further dominion? Everything has been pre-named, and pre-determined in such a situation, because the original symbolic premises have been accepted, and we have seen the extent of their entailment.

It seems clear that the arguments for and against symbolism are rather exactly balanced, even in the epistemological area inhabited by logical positivists. I am afraid we'll have to leave the discussion here in the state of a tie, to be broken in individual cases by individual discretion. So, for example, while a symbolic approach seems to work admirably well for the passage about Rebeca, where a symbolic interpretation seems to confer the only possible logic, this approach works

less well for the passage about Aureliano. In this latter passage, the only symbolic terms in which we can see 'where you
put your eye you put your bullet' are those that govern virtually all the utterances of a witch or prognosticator. Because Pilar Ternera is certainly that. She reads palms and
makes predictions which are astoundingly accurate, as the other
characters in the novel repeatedly discover, usually to their
chagrin. So what she says here is couched in the usual cryptic, symbolic language habitually employed by seers, from the
Sybil on up. But while we appear to be citing an example of
a useful kind of symbolism at work, we are really not saying
much. Because this sort of "symbolism," unlike that employed
in connection with Rebeca, is really too general to be of special aid to us in our attempt to understand the meaning of this
phrase. There seems to be a qualitative difference in the two
passages, such that the one is not only amenable to, but encour-
ages a symbolic approach, while the other is not particularly
enriched by it.

It is interesting to note (and we have just noticed it
ourselves), that in order to explicate the symbolism of these
two passages, it was imperative for us to go outside the passages. We had to explain that Pilar Ternera is a witch, and
that Rebeca had lost her mother early in life. Although a much
larger survey would have to be taken, many more passages turned
upside down and ransacked for their symbolic possibilities, we
feel on fairly safe ground saying that a symbolic interpretation involves a pushing outward, rather than a shrinking in-
ward. In other words, the ideas in a passage that function as
symbols, only do so with reference to a larger world, which
they represent, in contracted form. Even the initial application of symbolism is dependent on our being able to surround
a passage with a correlative framework. We don't invariably

think of the word "earth" in connection with "mother." Our
having done so here presupposes our having had some knowledge
of Rebeca's life history that couldn't be gotten from the passage itself.

This distinction is in a way similar to the one we made
earlier--that between the clear logical structure superficially
visible in a passage (the relations of the words on the page),
and another level of logical relations whose justification is
the "deeper" symbolic meaning of the words. Both of these mean-
ing-possibilities can be telescoped into an almost physical
"seeing"--that which is visible, and that which isn't.

Jacques Bens, in his afterword to Boris Vian's L'Écume
des jours, concerns himself with similar questions. This afterword is really a short essay called "Un langage-univers," which,
as it sounds, goes beyond a specific commentary on the novel itself and poses some useful thoughts about language and ontology
in general. Our distinction of the different sorts of logic
seems to be comprehended in Bens's opposition of the two words,
"mystère" and "mystification." As he says,

> Nous appellerons mystère un événement que
> nous ne comprenons pas et dont personne ne
> possède la clé; nous appellerons mystification
> un événement que nous ne comprenons pas
> davantage, mais dont quelqu'un possède la clé.
> Ainsi, si Dieu n'existe pas, la création est
> un mystère; s'il existe, c'est une mystifica-
> tion.
> On constate très vite (ou plutôt: on sait
> déjà) que le mystère n'est pas toujours
> surnaturel, bien au contraire: tous les
> phénomènes naturels restent des mystères tant
> qu'on n'en a pas démonté le mécanisme.[26]

---

[26] Jacques Bens, "Un langage-univers" in L'Écume des jours
by Boris Vian (Paris 1963), p. 178.

The mystère/mystification opposition digs even deeper than we
have done into the epistemological. We were working on the
level of the seen and the unseen, the known and the intuited.
But Bens has analyzed this distinction further, into the different ways of not knowing. Mallarmé might well find a peer
in this negative subtlety of Jacques Bens.

But what Bens is really opting for in this essay is a sort
of catholic view of symbolism, one that finally brings us back
to our two types of logic:

> . . . les écrivains ont toujours évolué à
> l'intérieur d'un même ensemble logique,
> ensemble régi, à peu de choses près, par
> les lois aristotéliciennes, et dans lequel
> le système des causes et des effets ne souffre
> aucune contestation. L'introduction de la
> féerie dans cet ensemble ne suffit pas à le
> mettre en cause: elle détermine seulement
> une sorte de translation superficielle, elle
> établit un nouveau système de rapports dont
> certains éléments diffèrent du nôtre, mais
> qui, dans son essence même, reste analogue
> à celui que nous utilisons tous les jours.
> Ainsi, les tapis volent, . . . des humains se
> transforment en animaux, . . . voilà pour le
> surnaturel. Mais ce surnaturel est inséré
> dans une trame parfaitement quotidienne, où
> les bateaux ont des voiles et non des pattes,
> . . . Autrement dit, l'existence d'une baguette
> magique une fois admise, rien d'inattendu ne
> peut plus arriver, aucun conte de fées ne peut
> réelement nous déconcerter.[27]

This is an ingenious view, if somewhat reductive. It
permits anything, because everything is potentially reducible
to uniformity. One sort of logic rules the world, from the
essay to the fairy tale, and symbolism here, instead of obfuscating, actually facilitates a series of translations and

---

[27]Ibid., pp. 175-176.

transformations. By that we mean, a man with three heads, in some mythical or fairy tale milieu, can be translated, in Bens's terms, into a very indecisive individual, someone who always has at least three opinions about everything (for example). In this perception of things, a symbolic interpretation is not optional. It is essential. Because being able to say that one thing stands for another is the only way of retaining the same sort of logic one depends on in everyday dealings with reality. Logic is the one constant in an equation in which everything else changes.

Not only is this view dependent on symbolism, but it also takes any specificity or uniqueness away from that to which it is applied. Bens demonstrates this in talking about the work of Boris Vian, giving the multiple symbolic interpretations critics have applied to the events and characters in the novels. It is surprising how many abstract ideas come from some rather concrete plot sequences. This multiplicity in itself should be enough to make us suspect any symbolic interpretation heralded as finite or conclusive. We grasp desperately at the ropes of a universal logic as we fall from the heights of symbolism.

But how does one prove that there really is such a thing as an all-encompassing logic, that is equal to any symbolic incursion? Doesn't that in a way limit what we can say, or even think? If everything at all magic or fantastic is just a variant of something else, something more conventional or concrete, then doesn't our thought have a very low horizon? We'd then have to feel that we've been condemned from the beginning of human life to structure language and thought around certain very specific categories, with a few die-hards making a last-ditch attempt to save the world via the fairy tale, poor doomed fools.

Another problem with the universalizing effort would come from an unexpected source--the language analysts themselves. If every utterance, no matter how fantastic, is automatically reducible or relatable to an area of a priori thought, then the position of these analysts would appear absurd. They would be left pointing mutely to the instantaneous transformation implicit in the "illogical statement." In other words, their contribution, by any standards, would have to be very much after the fact, the Old Guard showing a few sparks of interest at appropriate times, in its otherwise lifeless eyes.

The "automatic-transformation" view of logic and illogic seems destructive to all sorts of aesthetic enterprise, or to anything whose existence depends on figurative language or symbolic representation. Because quite simply, this view takes away from aesthetic expression its raison d'être, its initiative. If anything aesthetic is just a restating of a more level-headed reality, then why bother. It is certainly more effective and less time consuming to say something directly, without embroidery, and literature is nothing if not embroidery. An insoluble situation awaits us when we try to decide why we need literature, precisely how it is useful to us. The dilemma is compounded by the fact that asking such a question already prejudices any possible response. Just as literature might have difficulty responding to a demand that it be verifiable (one of the first things we talked about), it might also feel out of place attempting to demonstrate its usefulness.

What if we were to say that an illogical statement is a different way of perceiving from that of a logical statement? Wouldn't that create a logical reason to make an illogical statement? Admittedly, this sounds like sophistry, jeux des mots involving the terms "logical" and "illogical." But behind the word-play is a hardcore conceptual question awaiting

release: Are logical and illogical statements invariably interchangeable? Or do they differ in a way we might call ontological? It is just conceivable that symbolic (illogical,
imaginative) statements tell us something we can't be told in
any other way, because the _form_ of these statements is part of
the meaning. Non-literary, non-figurative language makes an
attempt, however unsuccessful, at reaching a level of trans-
parency at which the message, or content, can be exalted in our
consciousness and unimpeded by its transmitting medium. This
dream of clarity is rarely completely satisfied, but the pur-
posive bent of language of this sort cannot be denied. Whereas a poem, for example, does all it can to show us reality through
a tiny, crooked aperture, by using all the obfuscating language
at its disposal. Our view of the world will not be expanded
thereby, but it will be special, it will be subversive.

       To save ourselves, we might then hasten to make the tran-
sition to a positive world, to take a symbol and track it back
to its source, to surround a strange locution with the familiar
sounds of the language used to explicate it. (Explication always poses the implicit problem of simplification and rationalization. The soul of the poem is already lost as soon as we
begin to explain it.) But man's abuse of Eden doesn't change
the fact of Eden's existence. The _post facto_ explication, transformation, transubstantiation of a piece of imaginative work
doesn't alter that work. It rather shows that energy has to
be expended to wrench one logic from its resting place and lodge
it in another. And the amount of energy expended, the amount
of discomfort involved in this adjustment, testifies to the
strange originality of the perceptual aperture. But not, clearly, to the simply homologous quality of the two logics. It
would be unsupportable to say that there is no relation between
the different logics, because if there weren't, we would be hard-
pressed to view them both as logic. But the two logics differ

from each other at least to the extent that a translation differs from its original, and possibly more. A universalizing point of view often forgets or ignores this.

X

We might now turn to another question, that of private language. This is not a completely different subject, as it sounds, because in our discussion of the two types of logic, we were always talking implicitly about a form of private language. The logic of symbolism is not for public consumption: it is privileged, cabalistic, known to few or known not at all. In Chapter II we discussed private language in connection with a poem, The Rape of the Lock. At the moment, we want to consider the private language possible in a novel. In principle "private" language should be more accessible in the novel, because of the narrator and the complexities of his role; the fact that he is partially an author's porte-parole, partially an autonomous voice that must be reconciled with the characters and yet somehow differentiated from them. The balance is very delicate between what a narrator can know, and what he can't; the extent to which he is pure technique, and that to which he is intransigent material. These two functions of the narrator certainly account for the inconsistencies in the kind of knowledge we have of the characters; at certain moments, we seem able to pierce their souls, while at others, we barely see the outline of their actions. Finally, a substantial proportion of what we know about the characters comes to us through the narrator, through his lack of discretion. Almost every reader has at times had the sense that he wasn't being told everything, that something was being held back. Mystery stories are an obvious example of this, and equally telling is the impatience of those

readers who can't resist glancing at the last page first. In
this case, it is the plot that is at stake, but it is a plot un-
furled through the machinations of the narrator, what he chooses
to know about the characters' background, the reason they find
themselves in contact, the feelings they have about their more
or less painful and emphasized position, etc. While every liter·
ary work has potentially a narrator, as a way of disavowing au-
thorship and asserting its autonomy, this is partially a critical convention. One always feels safer saying, "the narrator
says," rather than "the author says," since there is no requirement that these be identical. But a narrator is at his most
active and resplendent in a novel (as opposed to a poem) because
a novel thrives on giving us a regulated amount of knowledge at
discrete intervals. It also exploits possibilities for different angles and points of view, while a poem usually concentrates
on immediate phenomena: an instant of strangeness.

The novel's own strangeness takes different forms. For
some reason (perhaps the passing of victorianism combined with
the upsurging of Gestalt psychology), the sexual initiation
scene has become almost a trope in the modern novel. The real
reasons for this fascination are obscure; perhaps they are simply a sort of wish fulfillment, a reliving of that moment of
surprised innocence in which for a second, everything seems
right, or everything seems wrong; the world telescopes and the
ego expands, until nothing is left but startled flesh. This
is a sort of idyllic, schematic picture of an event which doesn't
always have this crystallizing character, but which ought to,
or so they tell us. For the armchair sensualist, the real justification comes from reading about it in a novel, or even writing
such a novel, and this, even though the sexual initiation scene
obviously involves a certain degree of private language, which
to some extent vitiates or qualifies the necessarily voyeuristic nature of the account.

Contributing to the complexity is the fact that any number of paradoxical situations are possible in the novel, because of its insistence on showing us a kaleidoscope of angles. The most ordinary, nonfictional psyche is composed of so many contradictory facets of personality, the mutual expression of which would be terrifying, that it is not surprising to find pathological contradictions and paradoxes in a novel, which displays such a psyche over a collapsed period of time, and in combination with other, equally complicated psyches. Therefore, there is no such thing as a "simple" sexual initiation scene (although there may be certain clichés about it.) The reader is getting a highly distilled and very degenerate picture in such a scene, because he is seeing the internal and the external simultaneously, through the structuring lenses of his own experience, and in a more privileged, because less self-conscious situation.

Never let it be said, that Cien años de soledad is behind other novels of its time in its choice of scenes. The Buendía's oldest son, José Arcadio, is put through his paces for this purpose, and we will reproduce the scene at some length, since its quality can't be absorbed en deux mots:

> Entonces se confió a aquella mano, y en un
> terrible estado de agotamiento se dejó llevar
> hasta un lugar sin formas donde le quitaron
> la ropa y lo zarandearon como un costal de
> papas, y lo voltearon al derecho y al revés,
> en una oscuridad insondable en la que le
> sobraban los brazos, donde ya no olía más a
> mujer, sino a amoníaco, y donde trataba de
> acordarse del rostro de ella y se encontraba
> con el rostro de Úrsula, confusamente
> consciente de que estaba haciendo algo que
> desde hacía mucho tiempo deseaba que se
> pudiera hacer, sin saber cómo lo estaba
> haciendo porque no sabía dónde estaban los
> pies y dónde la cabeza, ni los pies de quién

> ni la cabeza de quién, sintiendo que no podía
> resistir más el rumor glacial de sus riñones y
> el aire de sus tripas, y el miedo, y el ansia
> atolondrada de huir y al mismo tiempo de
> quedarse para siempre en aquel silencio
> exasperado y aquella soledad espantosa.
> (pp. 30-31)

This is probably as good an initiation scene as any, to demonstrate the amount of private language that constitutes such a
scene. This particular one is so complex that it might be well
to enumerate its details, because it is really very sensitively
constructed.

To start with, there is the metonymy of 'he entrusted himself to that hand.' We have to remember that it is dark, and
a hand is the first thing José Arcadio brushes against. And
the darkness certainly heightens the effect of a disembodied
hand. Nevertheless, the statement about the hand is before
everything a perceptual statement, the importance of which is
shown by José Arcadio's being willing to entrust himself to it.
The whole passage, in fact, has a sense of passivity and ir-
responsibility about it, which in a way befits an initial sexual encounter. It is so strange, so different from anything
that has preceded it, that one doesn't want to take full responsibility for exploiting the opportunity. It is only afterwards,
when routine tightens its fatal clutch, that one can feel justified in repeating the history of the race.

The passage pushes on with this sense of passivity and
aimlessness. José Arcadio 'lets himself be taken to a place
without forms,' where they take off his clothes and do a number
of other things with him. It is interesting that many of the
verbs in this section are in the third person plural, although
there is presumably only one person, Pilar Ternera, who is doing all this prodigious activity. It is a stylistic device, as
its repetition shows, but it also is a way of emphasizing the

passivity of the passage, the sense for José Arcadio that he
is being taken over by unknown but powerful forces, which helps
him rationalize to himself his willing but noncomplicit participation in this act.

Not only is José Arcadio subject to dark and irresistible
forces, but he also finds himself in a region in which his normal physical abilities and responses are of no use: 'they
turned him to the right and left, in an impenetrable darkness
in which his arms were unnecessary.' All the physical parts of
José Arcadio not related to the performance are strictly de trop.
His confusion is manifold, since he first finds his arms unnecessary, later doesn't know where head or feet are, even more doesn't
know whose they are, and finally, can't understand how he is
doing what he is doing without a knowledge of the whereabouts of
his extremities. It would be an understatement to say he feels
disoriented.

In addition, his private trance goes beyond physical orientation problems. In trying to imagine Pilar Ternera's face (the
little woman behind all this excitement) he only manages a visual
image of Úrsula (his mother). This is certainly sounding like
the language of psychological symbolism. In that sort of language, there is always a tension between the public and the private, and for a rather simple reason. If there is any virtue to
Freudian psychology (and we are necessarily talking about the
Freudian, as opposed to the Gestalt or behavioral), it is that
our thoughts and actions, both waking and sleeping, have a logic
to them which is reflected in the concrete symbols that emerge
from our unconscious, and which we employ, even unconsciously.
In order for these symbols to be valid, they have to have a universality which transcends the individual. They have to be
recognizable in all their manifestations, so a meaning can be
assigned. This is where the tension comes into play. The

presumptive universality of these symbols doesn't accord very
well with their idiosyncratic occurrence in the individual.
The assertion of universality seems hardly able to survive in
the face of the infinite variations on the theme, the extremes
of which might be unrecognizable.

In a way, José Arcadio is in a classic situation. In the
midst of lovemaking, he can only see his mother. How Oedipal.
But is her image that of a mother, or that of Úrsula? Would
there be any visual image we could project on a screen and say,
"this is the image of a mother?" Of course not, because mothers
come in all packages, some of them surprising. So our question
reduces to whether or not José Arcadio is borrowing from a big,
prestructured psychological image bank, in thinking of his
mother, or is it simply that she is the only female form he has
known, before today?

The question is a sort of concretizing of the gross difference between Freudian and behavioral psychology. The first insists on rooting out the heart of the matter, judging precisely
what momentous childhood event could have been responsible for
José Arcadio's thinking of his mother at this critical moment,
while the other decides such information wouldn't be worth two
straws: let's take José Arcadio to a proper object, get him into action, and then see what he thinks about during lovemaking.
The treatment should either cure him or kill him, and that too,
is a solution.

Wittgenstein could never have imagined such an abuse of
his theory, but the difference in these two psychological approaches is a way of either opening or closing the possibilities
for private language. We said earlier that Freudian psychology
insists on a potential reservoir of symbolic thoughts and actions
from which all humans can, and do dip. This seems to argue
against private language possibilities. Yet in its orientation

toward specific, formative childhood experiences, this psychology
seems to be saying that there really is a private area to human
experience, with a corresponding private vocabulary which the
analyst can only try to elicit, by dredging deep into a presumptive subconscious area. There is at any rate a need on the part
of Freudians to bring things out into the open, which logically
enough presupposes that all is not plain to sight, that there is
an area of private language that even the subject himself does
not know exists.

Wittgenstein's objection to the possibility of private
language hinged on the paradox that if such a language existed,
it couldn't really be described in any conventional linguistic
terms, and that therefore it couldn't really exist, because a
language has to be describable. This is an almost irrefutable
objection, but we could say that a psychology which shows us the
existence of a private area not even known to the individual is
more or less confirming the possibilities for such a language.
At this unknown but existent stage, one could always assert the
presence of this language, without having to describe it. The
mechanism here is almost a temporal one, with the private language remaining in a state of suspended animation, continuing
to affect the subject while not being articulated, until the
analyst attempts to call it forth and put a name on it. By this
point, whatever it was he succeeded in eliciting would be highly
distorted.

Obviously, what we are discussing here (and psychology in
general) is largely metaphysical, just what logicians like
Wittgenstein spent their energies battling against. But on this
question of private language, Wittgenstein himself seems to have
opened the door to wild speculation, although he finally refuted private language on logical grounds which are unimpeachable.

We looked rather closely at parts of this private language section in Chapter I, so the faithful reader should know what we
are referring to.

In this chapter we compared the possibilities for private
language with the salient features of Freudian psychology--the
presumptive inner, private area of the psyche which must be
brought into the air, in the process of which, however, the
inner materia prima necessarily changes. To balance the argument, we were also on the point of saying that the impossibility
of private language is concretized in the orientation of the
behaviorist school of psychology. Again to oversimplify, one
usually thinks of behaviorism as dealing almost exclusively in
outward manifestations, with reference to both the problems of
the subject being treated and the cure. Thus the boy who suffers from an extreme terror when in contact with urine[28] is progressively exposed to it, first in minute drops, and later, in
much larger quantities until he succeeds in immersing his hand
in it, so gradual and confident is his habituation. No one
troubles himself about the causes of this strange fear, much
less its possible symbolic overtones. The problem is simply
dealt with on its own terms, isolated from any living temporal
continuum. For behaviorists, a problem of this sort has no his-
tory--neither individual nor archetypic. Its history begins and
ends with its successful treatment. While this approach doesn't
absolutely deny the existence of an inner, private world, it
certainly doesn't give it any importance. It says, in effect,
that all we can ever need to know about a human being can be
read in his actions and behavior. If this is so, if all the
essentials of a person are in full view, then the existence of
a private language would be ipso facto absurd. There would be

---

[28]An actual case history

nothing that could possibly merit being kept private--a locked safe containing play money.

To get back to our initiation scene, with the discussion of private language and psychology in mind, it seems that a combination of all these tendencies is at work here. José Arcadio is doing what many people do, but few of these reveal their feelings in the process. Fewer still even know very clearly what these feelings are, not even to the point of describing the extent of their disorientation in the situation. So in this respect, we are getting a privileged front-row seat at the theater of José Arcadio's private feelings. These feelings are made more private still by the fact that they are being narrated. Not even José Arcadio fully knows what these feelings are. But we don't even want to get detracked into that metaphysical morass. The scene is at the same time a devaluation of the role of private language (at least private language seen through a behavioral lens). Because in spite of the heavily symbolic, psychologically-loaded mother image, José Arcadio is finally only 'confusedly conscious that he was doing something that he had wanted to be able to do for a long time, without knowing how he was doing it.' Such a statement certainly shrinks the possibilities for private language, and argues for a blatant, cards-on-the-table behaviorism. Finally what José Arcadio is doing is what counts. His ideology about what he is doing is confused, and for practical purposes, worthless, except as a case in point to define the word "confusion."

José Arcadio's initiation scene is a triumph of the inarticulate. Of course, we can only see inarticulateness in a highly articulate context. It is a tribute to the author of this scene that he can create a character whose inarticulateness can be observed. It is clearly much more difficult to portray conscientious inarticulateness than the most polished discourse of

reason. A lot of distancing is required for this inarticulateness, because human beings put a lot of amour-propre into their
creations. A character who is neither more gilded and splendid
than the author, nor more titillatingly evil, is a real conces-
sion to the banal. Such a character at least represents a wasted
opportunity for wish-fulfillment, one of the only gratifications
still available to us in this overplanned and infinitely com-
passionate society.

xi

Whatever sort of character an author creates, there is always another dimension to, that of the imagination. Ryle's chapter on "Imagination," which we presented in Chapter I, has furnished us with a way of looking at imagination in literature which
is rather specific. Ryle's thesis is the limiting of kinds of
imaginative processes to those which can really be shown to be
occurring. He does not want us to be misled by linguistic formulae which seem to be asserting the existence of the nonexis-
tent. Ryle's function is therefore the retrenchment of inaccurate or irresponsible descriptions of imaginative activities.
While exercising this function, Ryle does, however, put us in
mind of many possibilities in the mental realm which we might not
have thought about otherwise. It is a sensitive account.

Alerted as we are to mental gymnastics of assorted kinds,
we aren't surprised to note that García Márquez has not neglected
this area of his characters' existence. Memory, prophecy, spiritual kinships of all kinds, are a major concern of Cien años de
soledad, so somewhere in this heap of qualities, imagination will
have to play a part. The reader who has intuited our rhythm will
know that at this point we have a passage all ready to show him.

Aureliano, having spent over twenty years of his life at
war, has come home again, at least temporarily, and has joined

the ranks of what is called 'a changed man.' We see this through
the eyes of his sister, Amaranta, who in looking at him, "no
lograba conciliar la imagen del hermano que pasó la adolescencia
fabricando pescaditos de oro, con la del guerrero mítico que había
interpuesto entre él y el resto de la humanidad una distancia de
tres metros" (p. 150). This seems to be a rather simple case of
imaging, where the present thing or person is contrasted with
a past memory of that same person's appearance. In this instance
the change not only of person but of character, is so great that
for Amaranta there seems to be an existential discontinuity.
What she remembers of her human brother has nothing to do with
this 'mythical warrior,' who for reasons of security has set himself apart from the rest of the world. The memory she has of
him is probably much more real than the way he must now appear--
as a sort of regal postcard image. In spite of this reversal--
the most proximate physically being the most distant spiritually--
this is a fairly clear example of Amaranta picturing her brother
as he was twenty years earlier.

The next example is slightly more complicated. It occurs
earlier in the book, with the death of Aureliano's child-bride,
Remedios. As a remembrance,

> Úrsula . . . puso el daguerrotipo de Remedios
> en el lugar en que se veló el cadáver, con una
> cinta negra terciada y una lámpara de aceite
> encendida para siempre. Las generaciones
> futuras, que nunca dejaron extinguir la lámpara,
> habían de desconcertarse ante aquella niña de
> faldas rizadas, botitas blancas y lazo de organdí
> en la cabeza, que no lograban hacer coincidir
> con la imagen académica de una bisabuela.
> (p. 82)

Ryle is, as we know, always trying to negate the conception that imaging involves having a real picture in one's head.
There would be no way to extract one's mental pictures and hang

them next to a real, external picture. So the above example is really to the point, since we (and presumptive future generations) are presented with a real photograph juxtaposed to our expected mental act of imaging. The two sorts of 'pictures' are clearly set off the one from the other in a comic way. Because the real great-grandmother, Remedios, since she died young, was a girl of about eleven, who naturally looked like an eleven year old. But of course the 'academic image of a great-grandmother,' is universally situated at about the age of 70-80, depending on the society's median age of marriage. So there is no way to reconcile the photograph, which is as faithful as the technological development of the moment would permit, with the 'academic image.' No academic image could really be correct here. One could also point to the obvious fact that Remedios' picture could be infinitely reproduced, while each person's academic image is 'impenetrably secret,' since there is no way it can be objectified.

It would really be putting us and Ryle to the test, if we were asked to distinguish between the photograph and the image in their ontology within the literary text. Because we have really been carrying on the illicit activity of speaking about the photograph as though it were a real photograph, which of course it is not. We don't have it in our hands; we can't look at it. With the image, it doesn't at all matter; images don't have a real existence anywhere. In effect when we read the lines of this example we have to imagine a photograph, as well as a standard grandmother-visage. So Ryle would probably answer that the whole example is a case of imaging, only one image might have a frame around it. But in strictly academic terms, the whole example has been of use to us in pointing to the difference between a photograph and a mental image.

Our last example is a more active one. It shows what happens when passive images turn pursuer. In this case, it is
Aureliano José who desires in the strongest possible way the
aunt who raised him. He goes to war to try to escape this sin-
ful cupidity:

> No había dejado de desearla un solo instante.
> La encontraba en los oscuros dormitorios de
> los pueblos vencidos, sobretodo en los más
> abyectos, y la materializaba en el tufo de la
> sangre seca en las vendas de los heridos, en
> el pavor instantáneo del peligro de muerte. . .
> Había huido de ella tratando de aniquilar su
> recuerdo no sólo con la distancia, sino con
> un encarnizamiento aturdido que sus compañeros
> de armas calificaban de temeridad, pero mientras
> más revolcaba su imagen en el muladar de la
> guerra, más la guerra se parecía a Amaranta.
> (p. 132)

The image of Amaranta is really being put through quite a bit
here. It appears in sordid corners of all kinds, the more sordid,
the more a guarantee of the image's presence. The presence of
this image has an active effect on Aureliano José's apparent
nature. In fleeing from the image in a self-annihilating way,
Aureliano José seems to be exhibiting a rash bravery which is
not part of his real program at all, but which passes very well
as a war mentality. As the ultimate act of aggression on the
part of the image, the war for Aureliano José comes to resemble
Amaranta. An hyperbole of this sort is surely the work of a
desperate man.

Certainly, we can still apply Ryle's theory to even this
extreme of "independent" image, saying that the entire pursuit
problem occurs in Aureliano José's head. That could certainly
be, and would be the psychological approach to the question.
That way, the image's credulity would not be strained; it could
undergo any number of transmutations in the individual imagination

perhaps endangering the sanity of the braincase's owner, but otherwise causing little harm. Ryle's way, though, wouldn't be the most grandiose way to go about it. Disembodied images, wars turning into women (think of Homer), figurative language that rises from the substratum and _is_ its own reality--these are just a few of literature's magic tokens. There are moments when the impossibility of an image's existence is not the only issue, but rather how convincing it is, how new it is, how far it can expand the imagination. At such moments, it is probably better to suspend all judgments.

CHAPTER IV
THE SYNTAX OF PERSUASION

i

In the preceding chapters we looked at a poem and a novel, using the insights furnished us by the language analysts, as well as a few of our own. It is now time to put the method to the test again, with a third literary genre, the play. Plays pose a new type of problem, in truth-value terms. Unlike most novels or poems, plays are written to be acted; speeches are made in which the speaker is impersonating some other entity. Fortunately, this thought does not constantly haunt us, because schematically, a play looks quite simple: the name, the colon, then the speech, clearly set off from adjacent speeches, tone, mannerisms, and situation all furnished by the stage directions. The play is such a whole-hearted and basically simple concept, that it is not surprising plays antedated poems in ancient Greece. The sense of ritual and community a play makes possible, particularly a play as chanted, is part of its allure. The Greeks were very aware of a play's cathartic involvement of a communal whole, and accordingly exploited the play's public possibilities, with ethical choruses which chanted the official point of view in any drama. The lyric poem came later and was a subversively private genre, the affirmation of the individual and an implicit affront to society, who, in the form of the chorus, felt it could and should be arbiter of all things. Private emotions, the stuff of lyric poems, were necessarily outside its domain, at least partially because they weren't proclaimed _alta_ _voce_ to the waiting ears of a thoroughly trained audience.

But the public nature of a play contains the seeds of its own undermining. Because nothing can be completely public and be literature at the same time, the act of a very private and very idiosyncratic creator. In addition, the very fact that a named person is making an affirmation is a sort of challenge to credulity. "Mr. President, what are your <u>real</u> feelings about the results of the upcoming elections?" Mr. President: "Well, I . . ."

Logical Positivists, like Frege, have talked quite a bit about the difference between direct and indirect discourse, and the way such a format affects the sense of a proposition (in other words, the difference between, "The goat is large and very potent" and, "He said, 'The goat is large and very potent'"). As in most of his logical thought, Frege is very precise about his distinctions here. He makes clear that there is a real difference in reference associated with the directness or indirectness of a statement. As he says:

> Wenn man in der gewöhnlichen Weise Worte gebraucht, so ist das, wovon man sprechen will, deren Bedeutung. Es kann aber auch vorkommen, dass man von den Worten selbst oder von ihrem Sinne reden will. Jenes geschieht, z. B., wenn man die Worte eines Andern in gerader Rede anführt. Die eigenen Worte bedeuten dann zunächst die Worte des Andern und erst diese haben die gewöhnliche Bedeutung. Wir haben dann Zeichen von Zeichen. . .In der ungeraden Rede spricht man von dem Sinne z. B. der Rede eines Andern. Es ist daraus klar, dass auch in dieser Redeweise die Worte nicht ihre gewöhnliche Bedeutung haben, sondern das bedeuten, was gewöhnlich ihr Sinne ist.[29]

---

[29] Gottlob Frege, "Über Sinn und Bedeutung," in <u>Zeitschrift für Philosophie und philosophische Kritik</u> 100 (1892), p. 28.

In other words, any simple statement like, "the chair is peri-winkle" has as primary reference an observable datum in the outside world. While making such a statement, one can theoret-ically point to such a chair, and thereby attach the language to an object. But in asserting, "He said the chair is periwinkle," we are not really talking about a chair, as we were in the pre-vious sentence. Our primary reference here is rather the _words_ of the other person, and _not_ the chair that they refer to. Thus we are referring to the sense of the words themselves. This referring to the sense of the words themselves is a little like Jakobson's definition of metalanguage, which we looked at earlier. It is again a way of limiting language's power, vigil-ing it from within, rather than always seeking some external vantage point from which to talk about language, permitting it unlimited autonomy of reference. Without such a theory of dir-ect and indirect reference, and lacking an object, language could conceivably go wild, making references to references in an infinitely regressing series, lacking any end.

But instead of peering at infiniteness, we want for the moment to profit from Frege's simple distinction between dir-ect and indirect statements. This difference seems to go a distance toward defining the way a play is different from, say, a novel. There is always an implied "he said" before each statement, and, even if we don't go so far as to distinguish between direct and indirect discourse, we still have a frame around each utterance which alters the ontology. This frame certainly affects the sense of each statement in a play, be-cause if Madame Choucroute says, "Modern medicine is a failure because it has never succeeded in effectively treating flatu-lence," we have to take Madame C's character, value judgments, habits, intelligence, and any number of other things into con-sideration before we can assess the validity of her statement.

This form of qualification is certainly true of all literature, to the extent that it is subjective. We don't want to limit the phenomenon to plays. But plays seem to be the clearest example of qualification at work, since, except for a few stage directions, our information can only come from what a character (or actor) says.

There seem to be two considerations at work in what we have said so far about plays, and these considerations go in two different directions. One is what we have just mentioned--the extent to which the statements in a play are valid and tell us something about the world. The other is what we mentioned in connection with Frege's interest in sense and reference--the implicit "he said" before each statement in a play, which can't help but qualify what is said. It is clear that these considerations are working against one another, since in the first, the emphasis is on the external reference of the statement uttered, while in the second, it is on the sense of the words themselves.

If we accept this implicit "he said" ("she said," "the priest said," "Mrs. Baldmutton said"), the demands we make on a play will have certain limits, in terms of validity and information about the world. One can, of course, refuse to accept these limits. But then the abovementioned research work comes into play, the examination of the personality, prejudices, etc. of the speaker of the words. Because even the most rigorous positivist could not deny that the words are attributed to some articulating entity, the person whose name appears to the left side of the colon. This research work is admittedly somewhat difficult if the speaker of the words is a fictional entity, as he in most cases is. In fact, trying to establish the identity of a speaker in a play is a big problem, and one which other types of literature don't have to the same extent. What I'm referring to, is the fact that plays are often acted, that

<u>actors</u> utter the words to the right side of the colon. This
fact, together with our problem of reference, makes the play
a complicated subject for logical analysis.

ii

Let's for the moment assume that we really are concerned
with the problem of a statement's validity. Let's take a hypothetical play, <u>Lost Worlds</u>, in which there is a character
Derek Jones, played by the actor, Charles Asherby. In the play,
this actor says "Science has just discovered that Mercury is
really the farthest planet from the earth, and that all the
others are optical illusions." With a statement of this sort,
almost anyone would be interested in knowing the truth about
it, even someone who wasn't a logical positivist. To establish
the absolute truth or falsity of the statement, we might simply
ignore the speaker of it and turn to the scientific means we have
available to us, which can probably tell us whether or not the
speaker is lying or misinformed.[30] But whether or not we want
to embark on this verification process in the first place is
often dependent on our knowing something about the utterer of
the statement, so we can decide if there are any real grounds
for this investigation.

In our hypothetical play, someone has made a statement
about the position of Mercury with respect to that of the other
planets. Who has made that statement? Was it the character,
Jones, the actor, Asherby, neither, or both? We might first
decide it was Asherby, since he is the person before our eyes
whose vocal chords produced the words we heard as the above-
mentioned sentence. But if it was, in fact, the actor, is he

---

[30]For an undaunted discussion of verification methods,
see A. J. Ayer, <u>Language</u>, <u>Truth</u> and <u>Logic</u>.

uttering something that is really part of him, or rather something he has been told to say? In other words, is he really making the statement his, by expressing it? A good actor manages to "feel" a statement to the extent that he can be said to have incorporated it. That is part of the magic of a play's staging. But of course an actor's empathetic abilities don't enter into the truth value of a statement, any more than does the color of the actor's shirt.

Here again, Frege has something germane to say on the subject:

> L'acteur jouant son rôle n'affirme pas, il ne
> ment pas non plus, même s'il parle en étant
> convaincu de la fausseté de ses paroles. La poésie
> exprime des pensées qui, malgré la forme de la
> proposition affirmative ne sont pas posées comme
> vraies; et ceci bien que le jugement et l'accord
> de l'auditeur soient sollicités. Ainsi, même
> si la forme de la proposition affirmative est
> présente, il faut demander si une affirmation y
> est effectivement contenue.[31]

Frege wants us to be sure not to confuse the form of a proposition with its actual content. An actor playing a role is in the privileged position of not being able either to lie or tell the truth, no matter what he says, because what he says only mimes the form of propositions, without having any de facto content. The actor is a neutral vehicle conveying a specious content. The only sense in which an actor's person enters into a statement's truth value, is in that which we mentioned earlier--the implicit subordination of the statement the actor utters. Thus,

---

[31] Gottlob Frege, Beiträge zur Philosophie des deutschen Idealismus 1 (1918-1919), quoted in G. Frege, Écrits logiques et philosophiques, trans. Claude Imbert, Paris 1971, p. 176.

while, "Science has just discovered that Mercury is really the
farthest planet from the earth . . ." may be an absolutely false
statement, one could assert with perfect veracity, "The actor
said that science has just discovered that Mercury is really the
farthest planet from the earth. . ." The subordination of the
main clause in this way removes the clause from the area of
direct reference, where it couldn't help but undergo the verification test. A direct statement offers itself to the world,
to be refuted, accepted, or ignored as the circumstances determine, but theoretically always open to judgments. And judgments
entail other things, among them temporality. Temporal qualification is the main reason even the "scientific method" doesn't
always hold true. A thousand experiments pointing toward a
seemingly indisputable result can all be overturned by a contrary result years later. So there is no real terra firma for
primary statements. Subordinate statements, as we have seen,
have almost unlimited protection against their being exposed as
frauds, or hailed as messianic. Unlike primary statements, subordinate statements are not complete thoughts; their truth or
falsehood is dependent upon the encasing primary statement. So
subordinate statements can never be put to the test. Their
real reference is indirect, as we have seen, so only the sense
of the words themselves is at issue. With no direct reference
to worry about, there is no truth or falsehood to be ascertained.

Frege himself poses the possible complication of having
a proper name in the principle clause which serves as antecedent
to a pronoun in the dependent clause. For example: "Hieronymous
Bosch painted idiosyncratically, although he himself thought
painting ought to follow historically-sanctioned lines." Since
the dependent clause here is so intimately related to the proper name in the principle clause, it is hard to know whether or
not this dependent clause ought to be exempt from truth value

considerations. To do the sentence justice, we might have to rephrase it into two separate sentences: 1) H. B. painted . . . and 2) H. B. (He) thought painting ought to follow . . . In this way we can see that there really are two distinct and independent thoughts here, both potentially subject to verification procedures.

With all this discussion of clauses, we have shifted the emphasis to where it rightly belongs--from the speaker of a sentence to the sentence itself. Certainly, that is a desideratum of language analysis, the beginning of the sort of objectivity essential to anything that attempts to be scientific in its leanings.

We had begun by discussing the very practical, non-theoretical difficulty of ascertaining the rightful owner of a statement, in some wild flight into biography. We saw that an actor's real responsibility for any statement is in doubt, even if he is the physical medium for its transmission, even if he empathizes thoroughly with what he is saying. Logic tells us that a fictional character can't be held responsible for his actions, even if they take the form of speeches which appear to suit his personality as we perceive it. The only being left to blame is then the author. But the author flees with the girl and the money when we consider he might not have used the statement for his own purposes. And even if he had, the context could not possibly be the same. So actor, character and author are alike guiltless and implicated at the same time. And, as a consequence, whatever statement an actor utters is neither true nor false. It is beyond judgment, both because it is an actor who is saying it, and because the statement has no direct reference. It is framed by "he said."

149

iii

So much for the peculiarities of the play as genre. What
about the play we want to consider in this chapter, Knock by
Jules Romains? The subtitle of this play is "Le triomphe de
la médecine," which sounds as though it will deal with a scientific or quasi-scientific subject. Actually, the play uses the
concept of medicine as a way of really talking about doctors,
following a long French tradition of 'mépris du médecin.' So
naturally, all judgments expressed in the play will be affected
and even structured by this particular bent.

But we don't know this at first, especially because, according to the stage directions, "L'action se passe à l'intérieur
ou autour d'une automobile très ancienne, type 1900-1902."[32]
There follows an elaborate description of the precise style of
the car, a "torpedo" as it turns out. And the beginning of the
scene is largely devoted to a discussion of the car's advantages
over newer models--the great amount of luggage it can hold, its
comfort and roominess. But at the same time as Doctor Parpalaid
lauds his car, stage directions tell us he is in a lower tone
urging his chauffeur to do all he can to camouflage the car's
manifest disadvantages. The object is soon in view; he is attempting to sell the car to Doctor Knock, who is being driven
to his new practice by Doctor Parpalaid. As the play continues,
we learn that Parpalaid has just sold his practice to Knock,
and some questioning on Knock's part makes it clear that the
practice is anything but thriving. As Knock says,

---

[32]Jules Romains, Knock (Paris 1924), p. 12. (All future
Knock citations from the same source.)

> La situation commence à devenir limpide. Mon
> cher confrère, vous m'avez cédé--pour quelques
> billets de mille, que je vous dois encore--une
> clientèle de tous points assimilable à cette
> voiture (il la tapote affectueusement) dont on
> peut dire qu'à dix-neuf francs elle ne serait
> pas chère, mais qu'à vingt-cinq elle est au-
> dessus de son prix.
>
> (p. 27)

Not only, then, has the praise of the car been an actual
part of the plot, but Knock's linguistic hook-up shows us the
figurative quality of this attempt to sell the car. Selling
the car has become a metaphor for selling the practice. Since
the play begins after the practice has already been sold, we
never get to see the actual transaction. But, to use another
metaphor, ex pede Herculem; seeing Parpalaid's attempt to sell
the car, we can imagine the unscrupulous methods he employed
to sell his medical practice, a much more serious undertaking.
Our point here is that a purely linguistic connection seems to
point the way toward an ontological connection. (We are not here
losing sight of the fact that the entire play is nothing but
language. But we feel that the action of language in the play
can conceivably illustrate the action of language in life, so we
permit ourselves to mention both language and ontology, and even,
to distinguish between them.)

Metaphor is a very important part of Knock (and of Knock).
In the above example it operates as an aid to perception. The
parallelism of Knock's sentence is an emblem of the parallelism
of the situation. So in this case, metaphor is more than a
literary flourish that brings two unrelated things into uncomfortable, if temporary, relation, as in the rosy-fingered dawn
view of metaphor. Metaphor here forges a highly logical connection, the broken-down car and the shaky medical practice are
analogous in themselves--they are both vehicles going nowhere.

And the two are also analogous in the way they are dealt with--
both are being foisted on an unsuspecting second party, whose
ruin if he accepts them seems assured. A lot of slick, adroit
lying has been going on in the sale of both commodities, all taking the implicit form "Doctor Parpalaid said the car runs well."
As we said earlier in our discussion of independent and dependent clauses, whether or not the car runs well is not open to
discussion in this form. The truth of the assertion is, however, cast into doubt in another way, by means of the more objective stage directions telling us of desperate attempts on the
part of the chauffeur to keep the car moving by any and all
mechanical means. Without the aid of the stage directions (a
play's compensation for its overt subjectivity), we could not
really establish the fact of the car's actual decrepitude.

A medical practice is certainly a less tangible thing than
a car. You can describe it, make a graph of it (as Knock eventually does), even take a look at a few patients, without really
being able to say you've experienced the practice. Very much
as Ryle's visitor to Oxford, who, after being shown the library,
administrative offices, and a number of other structures, asked
to see the University. In the Oxford example, Ryle was speaking of the category mistake inherent in this fuzzy view of what
"the university" was, and he was equating metaphor with that
kind of category mistake. But in this play, at this point in
the discussion, a metaphor is on the contrary a necessary vehicle
of knowledge, the only means of integration possible between the
concrete and the abstract. By means of stage directions, we in
effect can watch the car breaking down. But we can clearly not
do the same with a medical practice of some year's duration.
Therefore Knock's metaphor of the car's being like the failing
practice is not like the visitor's mistake about Oxford University. Knock's linguistic connection serves to unify the actual

resemblances between car and practice, both owned curiously
enough by one Doctor Parpalaid.

iv

The most standard, unpretentious metaphors can often serve
to illuminate real, but sometimes unsuspected connections. Thus,
in Act II, scene iii, in talking to the pharmacist, Mousquet,
Knock says, "Pour moi, le médecin qui ne peut pas s'appuyer sur
un pharmacien de premier ordre est un général qui va à la
bataille sans artillerie" (p. 75). This certainly sounds like
an exemplary metaphor, but there is one difficulty. That is the
expression 'premier ordre.' In order for this to be a perfectly
regular metaphor, it has, by definition, to include two discrete
areas of concern, which are then linguistically linked together
in a way that makes us see the epistemological fruitfulness of
the connection. Since the two parts of the metaphor come from
two unrelated worlds, their being joined together is a highly
arbitrary existential fact, a language construct the richness of
whose blossoming is only evident afterwards. This is a standard
argument for poetry's value to epistemology: it teaches by the
peculiarity of its juxtaposition, which the reader can then ac-
knowledge and meditate on, if he has not already rejected the
entire concept of indirect teaching.

In case the reader has not already intuited it, the sort
of nutshell argument for poetry we just presented is one of the
raisons d'être for this book's having been written. We save the
grand and dazzling tie-ups between literature and logical positivism for the end of the book, just suggesting here the possible
coalescence of the two worlds.

But to return to our metaphor, which has all the ingredients
of a good and unambitious language operation. Knock is comparing a pharmacist to the artillery of a general. 'A doctor who

can't lean on a pharmacist of the first rank is a general who
goes to battle without artillery.' There are a few things to
notice about this metaphor. One is that the doctor is not <u>like</u>
a general . . ., he <u>is</u> a general. The statement is more forceful
without the like or as, and suggests something between a mission-
ary and a crusader, a doctor who is both healer and inflictor of
wounds. Another thing to notice is the working of language within the metaphor itself. Knock feels a doctor ought to be able
to "lean on" a pharmacist. This is a colloquial expression for
having confidence in someone, or being dependent on someone.
In its literal form, "lean on" is much more of a concrete, physical verb than Knock is intending it. But it is hard to notice
this discrepancy in the heat of a battle metaphor. And speaking
of battle metaphors, 'premier ordre' certainly sounds very much
like a military term denoting rank. But the strange thing is
that 'premier ordre' appears in the part of the metaphor which
has not yet turned military. Knock is either anticipating the
second half of his sentence, or else making a Freudian sort of
connection, in using this adjective for the pharmacist. In
either case, the use of it violates in some measure the purity
of this metaphor, the sharpness of its lines.

It is not enough of a blemish, however, to spoil the
metaphor's efficacy as a source of new illuminations. Medicine
as battleground is not a connection we necessarily make every
day. But even at this point in the play, the use of this particular metaphor throws light onto the play's entire strategy.
Because it is obvious that for Knock to succeed in the inauspi-
cious practice he ill-advisedly bought, he will be forced to
treat the situation as a battle to be won or lost, surrounding
himself with allies wherever possible.

V

Up to now, we've given examples of metaphors which serve as clarification and advancement of knowledge. But not all the metaphors in Knock operate in this way. Some function in precisely the opposite way, as obfuscation and as category mistakes, in Ryle's sense of the term. There is, in fact, one category mistake which is an integral part of the plot. While gradually telling Knock the sad news about the practice he has just bought, the Parpalaids are themselves surprised by Knock's casting doubt on the fact that he is a doctor. Parpalaid was under the impression that Knock hadn't practiced before, because his medical studies were very recent. But Knock had in fact begun practicing twenty years earlier. Parpalaid naturally asks Knock for an explanation, and is given the following:

> En me promenant sur le port, je vois annoncé qu'un
> vapeur de 1700 tonnes à destination des Indes
> demande un médecin, le grade de docteur n'étant
> pas exigé. Qu'auriez-vous fait à ma place? . . .
> Moi, je me suis présenté. Comme j'ai horreur des
> situations fausses, j'ai déclaré en entrant:
> "Messieurs, je pourrais vous dire que je suis
> docteur, mais je ne suis pas docteur. Et je vous
> avouerai même quelque chose de plus grave: je ne
> sais pas encore quel sera le sujet de ma thèse."
> Ils me répondent qu'ils ne tiennent pas au titre
> de docteur et qu'ils se fichent complètement de
> mon sujet de thèse.
>   (pp. 32-33)

Knock then goes on to say that for reasons of respect and discipline, he would, however, like to be called "doctor" on board, after which he tries to justify the claiming of titles to which one has no right.

Here, Knock is obviously exploiting for his own purposes the confusion caused by the dual use of the term "doctor," for medical doctor and doctor of letters. He was, as he told the

Parpalaids, almost a doctor of letters; although he had a great
amateur interest in medicine. Being unemployed, Knock saw the
ship's advertisement and took it very literally. They were
asking for a 'médecin, le grade de docteur n'étant pas exigé.'
   This distinction doesn't work as well in English, where
"doctor" is used for both the practitioner, "médecin," and the
title, "docteur." Theoretically, in French there should be no
confusion about the difference. For Knock, there is no confusion. He is lucidity itself. Since he is neither médecin, nor
docteur, but is on the way to becoming a doctor of letters, he
can say with perfect probity, 'Messieurs, je pourrais vous dire
que je suis docteur, mais je ne suis pas docteur . . . et je ne
sais pas encore quel sera le sujet de ma thèse.'
   In order to gain employment, Knock is employing a method
both simple and subtle at the same time. The simple fact of
what he is doing in talking to the ship's officers is suppressing
the term "médecin," and subsuming it under the title "docteur."
In doing this, Knock is getting a lot of mileage out of the
clause, 'le grade de docteur n'étant pas exigé.' Obviously,
what the ship people are looking for is a competent, practicing
médecin; they don't care about honorifics. And Knock is not
lying when he says he is not a doctor. But nowhere does he
mention he is not a médecin, either. He has shifted attention
to the legalistic question of titles, so as not to be questioned
about the practical issue of his competence. The ship's officers naturally assume that his being a médecin "goes without
saying."
   Knock's very careful use of language in this connection
is more an example of metonymy than of metaphor in the classical
sense. Metonymy could, however, be considered a special case
of metaphor, since in metonymy, a part stands for the whole,
while in metaphor, something stands for something else. Whether

we class metonymy with metaphor here doesn't matter. What is
important is the category mistake, and the treachery of language
which permits this perpetration of fraud. Knock is forcing the
title of "docteur" (with its concomitant confusion of fields)
to stand for and take the place of the concept of "médecin."
"Médecin" is certainly more all-encompassing than "docteur,"
since the one connotes decades of early-morning baby deliver-
ies, injections, chest-poundings, anti-venom treatments, etc.,
while the other is simply society's acknowledgement that all
this activity is being done by a recognized practitioner. So
the two terms are really not interchangeable, at least in French.
Docteur is also used, of course, as the form of polite address
to a médecin. Here again, it is a mere title, like madame.

But in using the terms as though they were in fact interchangeable, Knock is committing a category mistake. To be exact, he is really committing two category mistakes. In the first,
Knock is blurring the distinction between doctor of letters and
medical doctor, in a simultaneous attempt not to lie and not to
tell the truth. In the second, he is also blurring the distinction we have just established (and which was to some extent in-
timated in the play), between "Docteur" and "médecin." Since
these are both very conscious category mistakes, with a desired
end in mind, we cannot blame their presence on unclear thinking.
And they do, in fact, further the plot, in the way cradle switch-
ing and partial deafness further Gilbert and Sullivan plots.

In spite of all that can be said in their favor, they are
still examples of how prone language is to inaccuracies, and the
frequency with which figurative language is apt to violate conceptual boundary lines in a potentially confusing way. That
is the other side of metaphor, the side language analysts dread
and fear. In the pursuit of comedy and surprise, writers like
Jules Romains dare brave the displeasure of these analysts.

After all, almost any metaphor when pushed too far verges on or
becomes category mistake. And the sort of surprise that is
vital to literature often requires that kind of pushing. In
addition, we might say that it requires a very skilful, conscious craftsman to take these kinds of chances in literature,
one who approaches the problem with an almost conceptual sense
of language's capabilities and limits. Here, and probably elsewhere, pushing language to its extremes is not done in a completely idle spirit. Its justification can be found in the
pleasure we get from playing the game.

vi

Two more small examples of metaphorical category mistakes
ought to convince even a skeptical reader that this play takes
a lot of figurative chances, that it is not quite the "scientific" document one might have supposed from the title. The
first of these two examples occurs in the stage directions at
the beginning of Act II, scene iv: "Elle a quarante-cinq ans
et respire l'avarice paysanne et la constipation" (p. 82).
We might consider this a category mistake for readers only,
since it wouldn't be apparent if acted, and it would even be
hard to know how a metteur en scène who had read the play would
interpret the description for the stage.

Category mistakes, by the simple fact of being category
mistakes, are often hard to think of or imagine, at least for
those of us who agree to any extent with Kant's feeling that
thought runs according to certain categories by means of which
it is structured. Kant, of course, was specifically talking
about spatio-temporal categories, but linguistic categories
might be considered to make a similar claim on our ratiocination.
This stage direction, short as it is, makes at least two category mistakes which we would find difficult to justify in

logicoanalytical terms. The one involves objects which are inappropriate to the verbs governing them, and the other is a
question of the lack of parallel structure. Thus "avarice"
and "constipation" could hardly be considered the usual objects
of the verb, "breathe," yet that is just what the grammatical
form implies. One would be in serious medical difficulties if
avarice and constipation were in fact what one was breathing,
instead of air, the odor of garlic, etc. The second category
mistake is contained within the first. Even accepting for the
moment that "avarice" and "constipation" could be bona fide
objects of the verb "breathe," there is something unsettling
about the juxtaposition of these two objects in themselves.
Avarice, as we all know, is one of the seven or eight thousand
deadly sins. It is an abstract quality that sums up in one
word years of stinginess, "making do," extraordinarily careful
secreting of money, etc. The word in itself, being abstract,
means nothing, except as the sum of all these daily, ingrained
practices. Constipation, one hardly needs mention, is a noun
of an entirely different sort. It is concrete to the extent
that it is capable of causing pain. It can also be relieved
within a few hours. One would hardly assert the same thing of
avarice, which is a chronic disease. In any case, it is clear
that the logic responsible for these sorts of word juxtapositions is not that which governs the language of the outside
world.

vii

We talked in the previous chapter about possibilities for
the existence of two different logics. There we were concentrating specifically on a "paralogic" of symbolism, one that would
make seemingly magical evocations fully comprehensible, once
one had accepted the premise that these magical events were

really symbols of the most quotidian details of life. The magical once accepted as governing order of the day, no further justification was necessary for anything that happened.

The attractiveness and the danger of this sort of reasoning are almost equally balanced. What is attractive is the degree of laissez-faire this kind of thinking permits. Virtually everything in literature can be justified if we refer it to some higher court of logic, to some profound level of organization. The danger of "separate but equal" logical spheres follows logically from its attractions. It is the problem of too much freedom, leading, as ethical philosophers and politicians tell us, to chaos. An infinity of discrete logics is surely a mockery of the concept itself. Yet literature's entitlement to its own, specific logic continues to charm discoursers on language and aesthetics. One such is Luis Núñez Ladeveze, who, in his work, Crítica del discurso literario, devotes a number of different chapters to the different types of logic. The one which he calls "Lógica de la Ambigüedad," is of most interest to us here. He describes it as,

> la lógica de la evocación, potenciadora de los
> contenidos evocativos de los términos con el
> objeto de llegar, no mediante una estructura
> silogística, sino una estructura particular, a
> una conclusión antropomorfa, no especulativa
> . . . una lógica de los contenidos evocativos
> debe precisar la ambigüedad connotativa del
> lenguaje para introducir un máximo de
> antropomorfidad en un mínimo de abstracción . . .
> Sus contenidos peculiares la sujetan a las
> prescripciones de una estructura lógica
> adecuada a sus intenciones, a su sentido
> antropocéntrico, a su contenido dramático.
> En este ambiente es más importante la
> sugestión que la exactitud, la analogía que la
> certeza, la metáfora que el ejemplo. Su objeto
> no es dominar la precisión generalizadora del
> concepto o del término que lo expresa, sino, por

160

> el contrario, liberar su plenitud evocadora, la
> carga subjetiva, dramática y flotante que
> comporta: el deliberado fortalecimiento de la
> latente ambigüedad de la palabra.[33]

What Núñez Ladeveze is doing here is juxtaposing the sort of
literary logic, which tends toward the particular and the an-
thropomorphic, to something like formal logic, which is much
more concerned with the general as embodied in concepts.

If we are to agree with this point of view, we would have
to be willing to sacrifice quite a bit for it. The emotion-
laden, the idiosyncratic, the self-indulgent, would always pre-
vail over the orderly, the repeatable, and almost, the describable. Because in order to describe with any clarity, a shared
and pre-existing vocabulary is necessary. Abandoning oneself
to the most extreme flourishes of the subjective imagination
would be like attempting to describe on earth a color one has
only seen on the moon, in some totally new color spectrum. Both
activities seem doomed to solipsism, and it is abusing the meaning of the word "logic" to assign it this restricted a compass.
Maybe "logic," or "logic of ambiguity," as used by Núñez Ladeveze,
is itself a metaphor for the type of approach one should make
toward literature, the sort of openness and receptivity that
are necessary in the face of literature's peculiarities. Unless
we choose such an eclectic interpretation for this kind of
logic, it is difficult to see how "the logic of ambiguity" can
be anything but a contradiction in terms. The "ambiguity of
logic" is certainly a much more meaningful phrase which does not
violate the existence of an ordering structure, even if it questions its univocity.

---

[33]Luis Núñez Ladeveze, Crítica del discurso literario
(Madrid 1974), pp. 70-71.

But we didn't come here to lose ourselves in terms, said
Dante, gingerly brushing aside the acacias. We are rather trying to rise to the challenge of a new way of looking at literature, a new way that is required by the thrown-down gauntlet
of logical positivism. This is and has been our working attitude throughout the book: half strain, and half confidential
expectation. "The logic of ambiguity" seems to be just this
type of composite--an unfinished tool for the ordered analysis
of literature.

viii

We promised, some pages ago, to give two examples of metaphorical category mistakes from <u>Knock</u>. We did, in fact, only
discuss one--that of the poor lady who was both constipated and
avaricious. (With time, and habituation, both qualities begin
to feel like the same thing. Any Freudian will tell you that
with his eyes closed.) It is lucky that we didn't yet disclose
our second example, because it suddenly seems very appropriate
following our discussion of the different types of logic. To
avoid any further suspense, our example comes from Act I, scene
i, and its context is the discussion between Parpalaid and wife
on the subject of the doctor's career plans. Knock is present,
and the tone of the whole is still governed by Parpalaid's desire to get rid of his practice at any cost:

> Mme. Parpalaid: Mon mari s'était juré de
> finir sa carrière dans une
> grande ville.

> Le docteur: Lancer mon chant du cygne sur
> un vaste theatre! Vanité un peu
> ridicule, n'est-ce pas? Je
> rêvais de Paris, je me contenterai
> de Lyon.
> (p. 18)

There is a figure of speech which is not appropriate here.
Keep in mind it is a doctor who is speaking. The doctor is
talking about finishing his career in a large city. 'Sing my
swan song' is obviously a way of referring to marking the end
of a career. There is nothing complicated about the interpretation; the only problem is the literal-minded one that doctors
don't usually sing swan songs--swans do, if we can believe the
biologists.

Clearly, this is again a metaphor, and a popularly accepted one. Swan song does not refer to the act of singing at
all, but means the moment of retirement from any life habit.
Again, we might hasten to say that this is metaphor as category
mistake. All the classic signs are there--the ascription of an
animal form of expression to a human, which is a violation of
a logical category. And as we know, category mistakes take many
forms, from the rather simple linguistic one of the woman in the
sedan chair, to the more complex conceptual one involving the
visitor to Oxford. But are we certain this is a category mistake? There is one doubt that we first have to allay. In addition to swan ponds, swan songs have been known to occur in the-
aters, notably, at the close of Wagnerian operas. In this sense,
and this sense only, can we find a sort of logic that justifies
what the doctor says and removes from it the "stain" of a category mistake. Because what the doctor is saying is being said
in a theater, where singing a swan song is not invariably an
abstract, figurative occurrence. We are in a way trying to adapt
Núñez Ladeveze to our own purposes. We are doing something like
turning his very general "logic of ambiguity" into something
like a "logic of the theater" here. Both forms of logic are
overindulgent to linguistic excesses; a tailor-made logic always finds some ready excuse for whatever indiscretion language
is committing at that instant. Our "logic of the theater" has

sprung like Athena from Zeus's forehead--fully-grown and ready for action. What more could a metaphor ask?

ix

The one thing more it could ask would be to be interpreted as something other than a category mistake. Never have we said that all metaphors are necessarily category mistakes. True, there are some that we would be hard-pressed to view in any other way. But many are open to a choice of description: category mistake, or an example of sense and denotation? When Knock asks about the possible vices of his new medical practice, and enumerates them--"Opium, cocaïne, messes noires, sodomie, convictions politiques?" (p. 43), there is no problem about whether or not this is a category mistake. It is clearly and hyperconsciously so. In this format, the reader would have to be blunt indeed not to notice the heavy irony of classing political convictions with something like sodomy. Making a category mistake of this sort is a technique often exploited by satirists of all kinds, and it is almost invariably effective. This effectiveness is only proof that we as language using beings have rather strong feelings about intuited laws of syntactic logic. Certain things sound right, even when it would be difficult for us to explain why. That is part of the pleasure and frustration of language learning, for babies and polyglots both. It is also essential for the appreciation of satire, or of anything else in which language distortion is a factor.

But cases of language abuse are not always as clear as this one. The man who said one man's sense is another man's denotation has yet to be born, but his spirit cries out for a more tolerant view of metaphorical language. A little bit ago we mentioned sense and denotation as an alternative to the category mistake, another possible way of viewing figurative

language. We think we can find in <u>Knock</u> a few lines that can
be offered as opting for sense and denotation, instead of for
the category mistake. These lines, coincidently enough, concern the same constipated, avaricious woman. She has come to
Knock for a free consultation, and he has, as is his wont, discovered in her a disease she had never dreamed of. But the psychological pressure of being told about the disease is such,
that the woman feels she must be cured. Common sense wars with
avarice, however, and she asks Knock the price of the treatment.
She is a farmer's wife, so Knock says to her by way of answer,

> Knock: Qu'est-ce que valent les veaux,
> actuellement?
>
> La Dame: Ça dépend des marchés et de
> la grosseur. Mais on ne peut
> guère en avoir de propres à
> moins de quatre ou cinq cents
> francs.
>
> Knock: Et les cochons gras?
>
> La Dame: Il y en a qui font plus de
> mille.
>
> Knock: Eh bien! ça vous coûtera à
> peu près deux cochons et deux
> veaux.
>
> (p. 87)

Knock always seems to have a sense of language that is
suited to any occasion. And this one is no exception. Knock
is trying very hard here to speak the language of his patients,
many of whom are presumably peasants and bourgeois farmers.
Livestock might be considered the farmer's specie. So when
Knock says the cost of the treatment is approximately two pigs
and two calves, he is not just playing with words. He is speaking in terms he fully expects will be understood.

This certainly sounds like a clear case of the difference
between sense and denotation. The denotation of discussing
treatment cost in terms of pigs and cows is still the absolute
value of the treatment, the extent to which it will reduce one's
income for the period under consideration. But the sense is
clearly not the same for everyone. Saying, 'this will cost you
two pigs and two cows,' would leave a classics professor cold,
or send him scurrying back to his Petronius. An ordinary businessman who wasn't in the fertilizer business might be equally
surprised, unless he could translate the expression into a joke
of some sort. Each of these two would need some other formula
for understanding the cost of their treatment--"That will cost
you the difference between your present salary and that you'll
get after your promotion," or, "That will cost you overtime
for four men for three weeks," etc. Farmer, professor, and
businessman now all understand exactly the cost of their treatment, by applying their respective senses to that one denotation.

In a society which believes in the instantaneous and demo-
cratic diffusion of knowledge, from the central computer to each
of the terminals, the learning process that involves all these
different senses would be viewed as cumbersome. Why not state
ideas in such a way that they can be understood by farmer, businessman, and professor alike? That is indeed, the desideratum
of radio speech and governmental documents. On the other hand,
a farmer and doctor seldom understand each other so well as in
the above-mentioned scene. It seems possible to make a case for
a somewhat idiosyncratic choice of expression, as Knock has done,
choosing to speak to the farmer in farmertalk, and, elsewhere,
to others in their respective jargons. It is one of Knock's
greatest talents, the single most important factor in his
phenomenal success with an inherited practice that was limping
toward extinction.

So there are advantages to the preservation of the sense
and denotation distinction. And even in terms of language analysis, which places exactitude before all, there is the acknowledgement that different people almost invariably have different senses of the same word. Frege, mathematical logician par
excellence, devotes pages and pages to the distinction, feeling
that much poetry and aesthetic expression comes from that area
in which identity of representations is not presupposed. And
while Knock is neither aesthete nor poet by profession, he does
not scorn to use those techniques of language which make human
discourse more interesting, and in some cases even facilitate
it. In Knock's case, metaphor comes full circle.

x

Knock is an extremely language-conscious play, as should
be clear from the amount of time we spent on the question of
metaphor. But of course metaphor is just a part of language,
and even though important for our purposes, is certainly not the
whole story. We all know that the whole story can never be
told, unless we find some other idiom in which to tell it.
That is at once our comfort, and our greatest despair.

Since we can't discuss the whole of language, we resign
ourselves cheerfully enough to concentrating on bits of it,
bits large enough to be significant, we hope. One such bit is
that suggested by Bertrand Russell, generally a good source of
bits. As he tells us,

> It is to be observed that words, when learnt,
> can become substitutes for ideas . . . Familiar
> knowledge is apt to be purely verbal; few school-
> boys go beyond the words in reciting "William
> the Conquerer 1066." Words and ideas are, in
> fact, interchangeable; both have meaning, and
> both have the same kind of causal relations to
> what they mean. The difference is that, in the

> case of words, the relation to what is meant is
> in the nature of a social convention, and is
> learnt by hearing speech, whereas in the case of
> ideas the relation is "natural," i.e. it does not
> depend upon the behaviour of other people, but
> upon intrinsic similarity . . .[34]

While the "natural" relation of ideas is perhaps a somewhat
dated, Platonic notion, or at least, one that is debatable,
the rest of the quotation strikes us as useful. It describes
a state of affairs that we usually take for granted, because
words and ideas are not that separable, and the former usually
manage to stand for the latter without difficulty or extreme
awkwardness. Nevertheless, in a play such as Knock, a distinction of this sort not only can be made, but is required, for
a complete sense of what the play is trying to do.

Not only is Knock in the grand French tradition of anti-
doctor plays, but it can also be situated in another, related
tradition--that of the "malade imaginaire." In that sense
Knock, or the Triumph of Medicine, is a real play of ideas. It
deals with medicine as an abstract concept, which doesn't ever
become satisfactorily concrete in the course of a play which is
ostensibly scientific. Knock isn't really a doctor in the plod-
ding sense that Parpalaid was. We see this, not from anything
Parpalaid does but from what is said about him by the people
Knock questions, while he is assuming his post. This extremely
clever listening, questioning technique is Knock's formula for
success. Success for Knock, contrary to logic and expectations,
does not reside in successful cures, inexpensive treatment, or
anything else of that ilk. It is purely a matter of amateur,
but highly polished, psychology.

---

[34]Bertrand Russell, Human Knowledge (op. cit.), pp. 110-
111.

Knock's first clever move, on beginning his practice is
to announce that one day a week, for two hours, he will give
free consultations. This certainly sounds like a false step
for someone bent on wringing centimes from a moribund practice.
But for Knock it seems to be a perfect beginning. In order to
make his intentions public, Knock summons "le tambour," the
French equivalent of the town crier. In the succeeding arrange-
ments, Parpalaid's past negligence is first revealed:

> Le tambour: (speaking about Parpalaid)
>   Et puis il vous indiquait
>   des remèdes de quatre sous;
>   quelquefois une simple
>   tisane. Vous pensez bien
>   que les gens qui payent
>   huit francs pour une
>   consultation n'aiment pas
>   trop qu'on leur indique un
>   remède de quatre sous . . .
>
> Knock: Ce que vous m'apprenez me fait
>   réellement de la peine. Mais je
>   vous ai appelé pour un renseignement.
>   Quel prix demandiez-vous au docteur
>   Parpalaid quand il vous chargeait
>   d'une annonce?
>
> Le tambour, avec amertume: Il ne me
>   chargeait jamais d'une annonce.
>
> Knock: Oh! Qu'est-ce que vous me dites?
>   Depuis trente ans qu'il était là?
>
> Le tambour: Pas une seule annonce en
>   trente ans, je vous jure.
>   (pp. 55-56)

One can see Knock's technique here, which becomes even
more marked as he interviews other members of the community.
It is that of a sympathetic, concerned listener, one who is very
easily surprised. In that way Knock learns a great deal at small
cost to himself. Success seems assured, as long as he acts in

a manner just opposite to that of Doctor Parpalaid. But Knock
has other tricks as well. One of the most useful is, as we mentioned, his idea of giving free consultations once a week. A
free consultation would naturally attract people who might otherwise stay miles away from any doctor. And because of his psychological perspicacity, Knock can't fail to make a "killing"
once such a person has entered his office.

The most celebrated lines of the play concern just such
a "killing." They involve the same town crier, who, after he
learns he is to announce Knock's free consultations, is very
anxious to have his turn immediately. Knock has very little
time, because he has made a series of appointments for that day,
to further his purposes. However, he accedes, and the town
crier begins to describe his symptoms:

> Le tambour: Quand j'ai dîné, il y
> a des fois que je sens une
> espèce de démangeaison ici.
> Ça me chatouille, ou plutôt,
> ça me grattouille.
>
> Knock, d'un air de profonde concentration:
> Attention. Ne confondons pas.
> Est-ce que ça vous chatouille,
> ou est-ce que ça vous grattouille?
>
> Le tambour: Ça me grattouille. Mais ça me
> chatouille bien un peu aussi . . .
>
> Knock: Ça vous fait mal quand j'enfonce
> mon doigt?
>
> Le tambour: Oui, on dirait que ça me
> fait mal.
>
> Knock: Ah! ah! (Il médite d'un air
> sombre.) Est-ce que ça ne vous
> grattouille pas davantage quand
> vous avez mangé de la tête de
> veau à la vinaigrette?

> Le tambour: Je n'en mange jamais. Mais
> il me semble que si j'en
> mangeais, effectivement, ça
> me grattouillerait plus.
>
> Knock: Ah! ah! très important . . .
> (pp. 62-63)

One could hardly worry about the gravity of the town crier's
symptoms. He certainly isn't going to die the day after tomorrow.
But his symptoms are, in fact, of a very special kind--the free
consultation kind. By this we mean the kind of symptoms one
thrusts forth and enriches at a free consultation, but which
one would never pay a doctor eight francs to look at. In short,
these are imaginary, or quasi-imaginary problems. And in this
particular case, in addition to being imaginary, these are linguistic problems. The difference between "chatouille" and
"grattouille"(tickling and scratching), is almost negligible,
particularly when the terms are being applied to imaginary symptoms. But the difference such a distinction will make in Knock's
income over a period of time is incalculable. The joy of dwel-
ling deliciously upon the infinitesimal details of his imagined
disease must be a heady one to the tambour, who has probably
not been paid attention to in thirty years. He certainly throws
himself willingly enough into the game, trying very seriously
to make a scientific distinction between "chatouille" and
"grattouille,"which incidently makes a very nice juxtaposition
in French. Even more ludicrously, when Knock asks him if the
scratching gets worse when he eats head of veal "au vinaigrette,"
the tambour responds that he never eats it, but that if he did,
he imagines it would make the scratching worse. Knock then responds, 'ah, very important.'

The entire scene is an absolute parody, both of traditional
doctor-patient roles, and of scientific attempts to describe the
self and its processes. This section is an unwitting demonstration of Wittgenstein's view of private language. The tambour

would have great difficulty even describing to himself whether
he felt a tickling or a scratching, partially because it is not
a real sensation he is having, and partially, that language itself is not exact enough.

xi

This is unequivocably a comic section, and the serious
attention to the diagnostic difference between chatouille and
grattouille can only make the tambour appear ridiculous. Yet
if we can manage to look at this part of the play seriously for
a minute, we will see language's apparent limitations. Language
often seems to fall disappointingly short of accurately reflecting or describing some reality external to it, whether it be external or internal to the speaker. If the object of language
happens to be some external datum of existence, we can beguile
ourselves with the hope that many different speakers concerning
themselves with that datum might succeed in approaching it, by
narrowing the field of untried phonemes. That, for example, is
what philosophy has been doing all these years, trying to satur-
ate the world of sense (and nonsense) with language that strives
to be increasingly exact, increasingly free of perceptual error.

One might be tempted to say here, that there then must be
a history to these attempts at transcending the omnipresent lump
of thingliness, that there is a certain progress implied in
stepping over the linguistic corpses of innumerable philosophers.
But the problem with this view is that it is difficult to imagine how historical progress could be possible for something
lacking in real content, like philosophy and like language.
It is even imprecise to put philosophy and language in the same
category, because language is philosophy's instrument, facili-
tation, and sine qua non. And certainly that is true of language with respect to any areas human thought has made subjects

of. There is not one field of human thinking that has succeeded in freeing itself from language, taking the word "language" in its broadest sense. That includes the most abstruse mathematics, and sciences that depend heavily on computers, which we know have "their own" languages, which function according to strictly logical laws. So language is a special case. Language as a subject can never be depleted, since writing about it just furnishes it with new material. It is a little like the principle of the carrot on the stick, affixed to the halter of the donkey pulling a load (of carrots?). Language is excused from the jury on linguistic grounds.

But then what about philosophy? It is neither, like language, strictly an instrument (think about ethics, for example), nor, like science, has it its own subject matter (think about how one would prove that a particular course of action was morally good). David Pears, in his introduction to Wittgenstein, puts the problem more clearly:

> Philosophy is not a science, but it has always existed rather ambiguously on the fringe of science. So when it is conceived as the direct investigation of thought, it is necessary to draw a firm line between it and psychology, and when it is conceived as the investigation of thought through the intermediary of language, it is necessary to draw a firm line between it and the science of linguistics.
> How are these lines to be drawn? If philosophy cannot move beyond other modes of thought into an area of its own, how will it maintain its independence?[35]

For answer, Pears goes back to Kant's idea that speculative philosophy can "serve as notional points of reference, which

---

[35] David Pears, Wittgenstein (London 1971), p. 28.

lie outside the system of factual knowledge, and so can be used to orient it."[36]

This is a rather abstract description of what is peculiar to philosophy, what distinguishes it from science. But Pears gives an even better example of the difference, again starting with Kant as his point of reference:

> Suppose, . . . that Kant was right in regarding causality not as an objective feature of reality, but as a kind of grid imposed on reality by the mind which views it: even so, much of the philosophical investigation of causality would remain unaltered. This may seem incredible, because, if a scientist became convinced that what he saw through his microscope was an effect of a flaw in the lens, he would start all over again. But the analogy is imperfect at the essential point. A microscope yields one set of observations, whereas what comes through the lens of the mind is the totality of human experience. So in this case there is no possibility of sidestepping, and no independent check, . . . When the field is extended to the limit, there does not seem to be any possibility of discovering that thought and reality might fail to fit one another.[37]

This seems to be a very simple and unusually neat way of emphasizing the differences between philosophy and science. It is evident that for science, what is important is content, and the instruments that tell us about this content. If an instrument is discovered to be inaccurate in some way, that is an extremely grave matter. All the amassed information that was gathered with the aid of this particular instrument is in danger of being discredited. One can hardly say the same thing of philosophy and its instrument, language. Because although we

---

[36] Ibid., p. 29.

[37] Ibid., pp. 30-31.

have all at times felt that language was inadequate to what we were trying to describe, there doesn't yet seem to be a better way of going about it. Again, it is the same problem. It would be hard to show that our language was inadequate for the purpose we assigned to it, because we'd have to show the deficiency by means of language. Even if we perceived something that we felt was not right with reality, what would be our method of indicating it? How could we tell anyone else about it? Pushing this problem even slightly immediately situates us in some absurd area, where reality is grotesquely larger or smaller than the language which is our approach to it and our power over it. In short, in any dialectical situation (and this is our best explanation so far for what language is with respect to reality), saying that language isn't functioning well makes no sense at all, except as a sort of metaphysical _jeu des mots_.

In actual practice, as Whorf tells us, our perception of reality accomodates itself to the language at hand, so that there is no possibility of jarring inconsistencies. Whorf's demonstration of this is striking:

> There is a yogic mastery in the power of language
> to remain independent of lower-psyche facts, to
> override them, now point them up, now toss them
> out of the picture, to mold the nuances of words
> to its own rule, whether the psychic ring of the
> sounds fits or not . . . What happens is that,
> when a word has an acoustic similarity to its
> own meaning, we can notice it, as in English
> 'soft' and German _sanft_. But, when the opposite
> occurs, nobody notices it. Thus German _zart_
> (tsart) 'tender' has such a "sharp" sound, in
> spite of its _a_, that to a person who does not
> know German it calls up the bright-sharp mean-
> ings, but to a German it "sounds" _soft_.[38]

---

[38]Benjamin Lee Whorf, _Language_, _Thought and Reality_ (Cambridge 1956), pp, 267-268.

This evidence of language's suggestive power to control perceptions might make us wonder about possible "ultimate bases for reality." This is of course, the area of metaphysics, the Unalterable Essence. But even if such an Essence exists, its means of approach are hard of access, particularly if we have to pass through the suggestible human range of awareness. How much more secure to put our faith in what we have before us, the language of men, rather than play mystical games in solitary channels.

But these sorts of games are what philosophy used to play, when it sought to transcend the sensible, or perceptible. And this is just what logical positivism and language analysis were trying to purge it of, this tendency to point magisterially off into space, with the conviction of a beyond which was ineffable or ungraspable. One could say that philosophy went wrong precisely when it attempted to have an object, to have content, to be the means to arcane knowledge.

The problem becomes more acute when we try to talk about a history of philosophy as one would a history of science. In themselves they are not at all comparable. Scientific discoveries are built one on top of the other. Invention of the microscope made possible discovery of the paramecium; the order could not logically be reversed. But it is not quite so crucial to know which philosophical argument came first. One argument may incorporate another in its refutation of that other, but it would be difficult to trace a direct line of theoretical perfectibility between them. Saying Carnap is better than Plato doesn't make much sense. One may like Carnap's style better than that of Plato, perhaps think Carnap's arguments are stronger, but beyond those rather formal criteria, a value judgment stating that Carnap has improved with time over Plato is pointless. Different ways of thinking about things are simply that--different. Looking at an idea in isolation, can we possibly know it is a more advanced idea than another, that it has benefited from its owner's having been born one hundred years later than another idea's owner? Probably not.

Emilio Lledo suggests one solution to the problem, which we would have to call the "marxist answer":

> Las ideas, como tales, no tienen historia, si consideramos al pensamiento como un ámbito teórico, como una simple formalización. La historia llega a las ideas a través de la presión que la praxis ejerce sobre ellas, y por praxis hay que entender, en nuestro caso, la presencia de las intenciones de un quién; presencia en la que se condensa la cultura, el nivel social, los intereses de una personalidad o de un grupo, en el que el lenguaje presta la imprescindible y determinante estructura intersubjetiva.[39]

Lledo's statement confirms the nonsubstantive nature of ideas, and to that extent, doesn't draw science and philosophy any closer together. It does, however, step outside the realm of ideas to their substratum--the human and social causes and bearers of ideas. And even though this doesn't directly solve our carrot-and-stick problem of modifying language through language, it does locate ideas in a seemingly logical area, that of intersubjective human cerebration. Philosophy from this point of view becomes one of the most pragmatic and entrenched of human activities, growing as it does directly out of the daily social life of human animals. Wittgenstein's term, "doing philosophy," also becomes more comprehensible, viewed in this way, like "doing the gardening," or "walking the dog." Insisting on praxis also confirms the absurdity of trying to separate

---

[39] Emilio Lledo, Filosofía y lenguaje (Barcelona 1974), p. 111.

language and reality, since language perforce grows out of
reality and modifies and is modified by it.

Such a view still leaves space for debates of the chicken-
and-egg sort: whether language is a picture of reality, implying some pre-existent, on the whole stable reality which it is
language's function to reflect as best it can, or that language,
in practice, creates its own reality, or at least, decides in
merely existing just what is important or necessary to say about
reality. There is no solution to this pretty well-balanced discussion. Different views find currency in different centuries,
sometimes with the aid of ancillary sciences like linguistics or
anthropology. And as we know from Wittgenstein's theoretical
change of direction from the Tractatus to the Investigations,
the shift in views can be even more rapid than that.

From one perspective, looking at reality as there to be
described has its comforting aspects. God created the world in
a stable way and there it is, we dance on its surface; our feet
never plunge up to the knee into some viscous and unfamiliar substance. In addition, in such a view, there is a finite amount
of material that language can help us to see; whether we encompass it or not depends on our own efforts. It is sort of the
happy-child-waking-up-in-the-morning-with-a-quarter-in-his-
pocket theory: the world waits; we have the means.

The idea that language creates its own reality is more
problematical in its philosophical outlook, but a lot simpler in
application. It is problematical because language is a human
product. And for something to be at once a human product, and
the furnisher of the conditions of human existence, is at least
awkward. It is difficult to reconcile the 'we create reality
through language' idea with 'we live in a certain reality' because there seems to be no stopping the freely-turning set of
cogs.

Ernst Fischer comes to our aid here, in a curiously parallel
discussion of the artist and society:

> Usually the artist recognized a twofold social
> mission: the direct one imposed by a city, a cor-
> poration, or a social group; and the indirect one
> arising from an experience which mattered to him,
> i.e. from his own social consciousness. . .
> generally, an artist who belonged to a coherent
> society and to a class that was not yet an impedi-
> ment to progress did not feel it as any loss of
> artistic freedom if a certain range of subjects
> was prescribed to him. Such subjects were very
> rarely imposed by an individual patron's whim,
> but usually by tendencies and traditions deeply
> rooted in the people. By his original handling
> of a given subject, an artist could express his
> individuality and at the same time portray the
> new processes taking place within society. His
> ability to bring out essential features of his
> time and to disclose new realities was the mea-
> sure of his greatness as an artist.[40]

What Fischer is saying here begins to feel like an answer to our
dilemma. The artist, operating within a set of socially-
sanctioned themes, yet conferring upon them his individual touch,
can be the model for the language that emerges from the surrounding reality and which also helps to form that reality, in the
idiosyncratic use of individuals. It is not a mysterious process.

In actual practice however, the linguistically-predominant
position may appear more conspicuous. Because without this emphasis, what analyzable traces of reality are there for us to
look at? By what kinds of prints or tracks are we to recognize
reality? Without language, reality crowds in on top of us; we
have no way to fend it off, because we have no means of drawing

---

[40] Ernst Fischer, The Necessity of Art (Middlesex 1963),
p. 47.

its shape, or even its outlines. How much more comforting to
lean on language in times of war or cataclysm, for example, even
if the dependence takes the paltry form of memos from the War
Office. If, instead of an harmonious integration, we are forced
to take one side or another in the language/reality predominance
question, then we prefer finally not to commit ourselves, and
this for two reasons: 1) Because of the nature of the subject,
whatever opinion we assume will probably be in opposition to
prevailing attitudes by the time the manuscript is published,
and 2) having adopted language as our means of negotiating with
reality, we feel we would not be able to arbitrate the question
fairly, without undermining our magisterial position. So we
waive our right to the last word. We do, however want to take
up the question in Knock, since it is unavoidable, and for individual works we are disposed to be partial, however much it
may cost us in emotional energy.

xii

We left Knock with the tambour describing the symptoms of
his largely hypochondriacal disease. That is, in fact, what
launched us on our large digression about language, philosophy,
and reality, so perhaps the tambour's disease is communicable.
(Another victory for the language-creating-reality view; nothing
is ever truly a digression.) The growing intensity of the tambour's symptoms under discussion suggested what we'll call the
linguistically-generative theory: reality-creation through
language. The tambour became progressively sicker with Knock's
questions, until finally, he felt genuinely ill. Although the
psychology of this operation is familiar to almost everybody,
one can still isolate the language that is responsible for the
tambour's psychological state, as well as that of Knock's other
victims. Quasi-scientific, or at least positive language, like

Knock's insisting, "Ne confondons pas," is partially responsible for the tambour's taking himself as seriously as he does.
Knock's "Désignez-moi exactement l'endroit," gives the tambour
a sense of purpose he may never before have had, the need to
specify as though his life depended on it. And if Knock has
his way, the tambour <u>will</u> think that his life depends on the
exactitude of the diagnosis. There is not a single, significa-
tion-bearing "ah!" which is uttered in vain by Knock. Each one
will eventually wring an additional eight francs from the tambour, who is only the first in a long series of more-than-will-
ing victims.

Knock has a number of techniques for inducing hypochondria,
and they are almost all linguistic. However, the world of gestures contributes to Knock's effectiveness. Again, the stage
directions of a play put the reader (and the audience, if the
play is skillfully acted) in a privileged position, giving us
a more complete sense of Knock's methods. Thus, a description
of Knock in a typical attitude is, "qui n'a cessé d'être par-
faitement attentif" (p. 94). What Knock is listening to hardly
ever justifies the attention, but that is one of the secrets of
the hypochondria business. Being an unquenchable listener is
essential.

Knock even manages to convey an air of sickness to people
who haven't come to him to be treated. In a discussion about
educating the masses to think about hygiene, Knock makes the
local schoolteacher, or "instituteur," feel very uncomfortable.
Innocent statements about the habits of the masses, like, "Je
parie qu'ils boivent de l'eau sans penser aux milliards de
bactéries qu'ils avalent à chaque gorgée" (p. 70), is the beginning of it. Here, Knock's deliberate casualness with respect
to his interlocutor, the implicit assumption that the schoolteacher himself takes precautions against drinking water,

signals the beginning of a subtle terror. This terror worsens, when Knock briefly outlines a mass reeducation plan:

> Vous arrangerez tout cela comme vous savez le
> faire. Tenez, pour débuter, une petite
> conférence, toute écrite, ma foi, et très
> agréable, sur la fièvre typhoïde, les formes
> insoupçonnées qu'elle prend, ses véhicules
> innombrables: eau, pain, lait, coquillages,
> légumes, salades, poussières, haleine, etc. . .
> les semaines et les mois durant lesquels elle
> couve sans se trahir, les accidents mortels
> qu'elle déchaîne soudain, . . .
> (pp. 71-72)

We can easily imagine Knock's saying these awful things in a very matter-of-fact voice, while the schoolteacher visibly whitens in front of him, even though these cautions are ostensibly not meant for him. This is again only language at work, but it is having its effect on reality. Because the schoolteacher really begins to feel sick: "C'est que . . . je suis très impressionable . . . Je n'ai pas déjà une santé si solide. Mes parents ont eu beaucoup de peine à m'élever. Je sais bien que, sur vos clichés, tous ces microbes ne sont qu'en reproduction. Mais enfin . . ." (pp. 72-73). By the end of the play, the schoolteacher is driven to extremes of hypochondria: "M. Bernard, l'instituteur, qui s'était mis dans la tête qu'il était porteur de germes et qui n'en vivait plus. Pour le rassurer, le docteur Knock a été jusqu'à lui analyser trois fois ses excréments" (p. 122).

xiii

Knock uses what is assuredly a diabolical combination of psychology and linguistic shrewdness (the two are close) to work his will on these and other patients, vignettes of whom we are shown. In his conversation with the pharmacist, Mousquet,

Knock's interests and objects seem more generalized. Up to now, they have been limiting themselves to inspiring terror in individual patients. But when Mousquet starts to complain about a lack of revenue, due to a lack of regular clients, Knock becomes animated:

> Knock: Par occasion? Point du tout.
> Client régulier, client fidèle.
>
> Mousquet: Encore faut-il qu'il tombe
> malade!
>
> Knock: "Tomber malade", vielle notion
> qui ne tient plus devant les
> données de la science actuelle.
> La santé n'est qu'un mot, qu'il
> n'y aurait aucun inconvénient
> à rayer de notre vocabulaire.
> Pour ma part, je ne connais que
> des gens plus ou moins atteints
> de maladies plus ou moins
> nombreuses à évolution plus ou
> moins rapide. Naturellement,
> si vous allez leur dire qu'ils
> se portent bien, ils ne demandent
> qu'a vous croire"
>   (p. 80)

This is, both for our purposes, and for the play's own argument, a central issue and sort of issue. Reading these lines we could legitimately ask ourselves whether language here is serving as a picture of reality, or creating its own reality. Knock is certainly doing a lot of brisk hatchet work with language, and then putting the pieces back together in just the way it suits him. It is a little like what the language analysts do when they restate propositions so we can see what they are really saying. Only, in their case they are doing it to establish the actual truth-value of the propositions, while Knock is doing his best to rephrase statements so they seem to be representing his exact ends. The whole thing becomes almost an ethical question--whether one can in good conscience manipulate language to this extent. Words like propaganda tend to surface here, and with reason. Knock is doing some highly unorthodox maneuvering, the direct result of which is personal material gain.

There may, of course, be genuine ideological or philosophical issues involved here too. It is hard to tell. Knock would not be the success he eventually becomes, if his views were not seen as somehow "inspired." Seeing the whole world as sick and in need of a cure has almost a Christian, or at least, a religious sound to it. And although that is probably asking too much from a play that is simply presenting a medical manipulator, there is a bit more evidence for this view. Toward the end of the play, when Knock is showing Parpalaid his triumph, not the least of which is the fact that, "dans quelques instants, deux cent cinquante thermomètres vont pénétrer à la fois" (p. 139), Knock looks at the town spread out beneath his gaze, a town filled with sick people, and says, "Le canton fait place à une sorte de firmament dont je suis le créateur continuel" (p. 139). This is admittedly a strange sort of religion, sounding more Nietzschean than Christian. But it is a tiny indication that Knock may have been acting with something other than self-interest in mind. (Either that or the most extreme form of self-interest--the self as god.)

But aside from this momentary lapse into divine reason, Knock usually bases his arguments on linguistic or scientific grounds. To return to the earlier quotation, the one which asserted, 'La santé n'est qu'un mot,' we can see that Knock's strategy employs human reason and the teachings of science. As we suggested earlier, the language analysts might go about their arguments in the same way. They might look at the word "health," and try to decide whether it is meaningful or senseless. They would probably rule the word out on the grounds that it is too vague, and demand instead to see an individual demonstrating all the signs of health. That then, would be health, incarnate in one person. So there, Knock and the language analysts would be in accord. But Knock's rephrasing, although clever in the extreme, might not satisfy them. Instead of applying the word "health" to human beings, Knock puts forth a pragmatic, or experiential argument: "It seems to me that everybody has a greater or lesser number of diseases which are in different stages of evolution." The French says it better, with more _panache_, but the idea is that, while health is only a word, a permanent state of disease is a reality. The disease may be hidden, may take a lifetime or more to develop, but it is nevertheless always there, _in potentia_. The trouble with this theory is that it is just as hard to prove as that of health's being just a word. Except in certain cases, where the symptoms are evident, the state of being diseased is as metaphysical as that of being healthy.

Knock makes argument even more difficult by criticizing the concept, 'to fall sick.' His supposed proof for the inadequacy of the term is that it 'ne tient plus devant les données de la science actuelle.' This has an impressive ring to it, no doubt. Even the language analysts might be temporarily appeased by it. Knock is obviously vibrating with the excitement of science's power and potential, which at the beginning of the twentieth-century was less alloyed with cynicism than it is now. We can see that by the brashness with which Knock elsewhere speaks of radiotherapy as a standard, very modern treatment. We can only shudder at such casualness, and agree with the language analysts that there is no such thing as eternal truth based on experience.

Knock himself seems properly conscious of this fact. In another part of the play, where Doctor Parpalaid comes back,

sees the progress Knock has made, and objects that 'you can't
put a whole population into bed,' Knock says to him, "Votre
objection me fait penser à ces fameux économistes qui pré-
tendaient qu'une grande guerre moderne ne pourrait pas durer
plus de six semaines" (p. 136). Always well-informed, Knock
here exposes the folly of a pseudo a priori statement, a theory
which was controverted by experience. And in spite of his calling on the 'données of modern science,' (which is in its own
right a pretty vague corroboration), Knock's methods seem to be
based on practice rather than theory. Science is fine, in its
proper place. But only as the handmaid of human linguistic and
psychological efforts. Never as a God. It is this attitude
which makes Knock the refreshing and slightly naughty play it
is. Knock them on the head with language, fell them with
phonemes, and if they are still obdurate, then call upon Science,
in a vague enough conceptual form, preferably with a capital
"S." But only when all the other options have been exhausted.

The denouement of the play is in this same spirit.
Parpalaid has returned to the town, noted that nearly everyone
was in bed, and naturally wondered about it. And we have seen
how Knock, by suggestion, treachery, even just force of personality, has worked his will on a number of individuals. So it is
not surprising that Parpalaid should ask Knock, "Mais est-ce que,
dans votre méthode, l'intérêt du malade n'est pas un peu
subordonné à l'intérêt du médecin?" (p. 134). And for Knock to
reply:

>   Knock: Docteur Parpalaid, vous
>   oubliez qu'il y a un
>   intérêt supérieur à ces
>   deux-là.
>
>   Parpalaid: Lequel?
>
>   Knock: Celui de la médecine. C'est
>   le seul dont je me préocupe.
>   (pp. 134-135)

This is a perfect stroke. It reduces Doctor Parpalaid to a meditative jelly, and bathes Knock in a resplendent, other-worldly light, like some sort of Aesculapian White Knight. And as the stage directions tell us, the lighting of the stage does at that point change, so as to reflect the new metaphysical order of things:

> A partir de ce moment et jusqu'à la fin de la
> pièce, l'éclairage de la scène prend peu à peu
> les caractères de la Lumière Médicale, qui,
> comme on le sait, est plus riche en rayons verts
> et violets que la simple Lumière Terrestre . . .
> (p. 135)

xiv

Before Knock disappears forever in a triumphal clatter of medical machinery, there is one more thing we want to say about this play, which is something we might say about any play, and which leads us back to the beginning of the chapter. There, we talked about the effect the implicit "he said" before each speech had on the speech; how the external framing of a statement affects the statement's message. We heard what Frege had to say on the subject, but since it has become our informal tradition to end each chapter with Ryle, we might eavesdrop on him a bit, too.

Ryle intersects with thinking about a play when he discusses pretending. Certainly a play is nothing if not pretending, projecting a personality out ahead of one. Diderot recognized this early[41] but Ryle wasn't that far behind him. Of course

---

[41]Denis Diderot, Paradoxe sur le comédien in Oeuvres esthétiques, (Paris 1959).

Ryle approaches the question from a different point of view,
that of a language analyst. As he says,

> To describe someone as pretending is to say
> that he is playing a part, and to play a part
> is to play the part, normally, of someone who
> is not playing a part, but doing or being some-
> thing ingenuously or naturally. . . The differ-
> ence is parallel to that between quoting an as-
> sertion and making it. If I quote what you as-
> serted, then what I say is just what you said;
> . . . Yet the full description of my action is
> not at all like that of yours. Yours was, per-
> haps, an exercise of the skill of a preacher;
> mine is that of a reporter or mimic; you were
> being original; I am being an echo . . . the words
> I utter are uttered, so to speak as they would
> be written, inside inverted commas. The words
> you uttered were not . . . In the same sort of
> way, while the bear just growls, the child's
> growling is, so to speak, inside inverted
> commas . . . A mock-performance differs from the
> ingenuous performance which it represents, not
> in being a complex of performances, but in be-
> ing a performance with a certain sort of complex
> description. A mention of the ingenuous per-
> formance is an ingredient in the description
> of the mock-performance.
>
> (pp. 259-260)

So for Ryle, pretending to be something else, or saying
someone else's lines, is the sort of activity that has to be
discussed in a particular way, since its genesis is in another
sort of activity. A good actor suppresses this distinction,
makes it very hard for us to describe the fact that there really
are two discrete activities in his performance. Yet epistemo-
logically, there always has to be, even though the stage per-
petuates the illusion of a fresh and unitary occurrence. As
Ryle reminds us, we might say of an actor impersonating a doctor that he is "convincing." But we would hope never to have
to say that about the doctor himself, unless we discover from
some damning act of his, that he is a charlatan. Those moments

where Knock seems to verge on charlatanism really challenge an
ontology-hunter's perspicacity. Acting a charlatan impersonating
a doctor seems unnecessarily complicated, and therefore very
contemporary.

AFTERWORD

It is uppermost in our consciousness that, without a bona
fide beginning, middle, and end to which he can apply himself,
no red-blooded reader can ever feel satisfied that he has done
a book (and himself) justice. Without being able to know that,
"in my beginning is my end," the reader may feel he is naviga-
ting in uncharted territory, where whales look like land masses,
and land masses are really whales. Less metaphorically, whatever conclusions a reader has drawn in the course of reading,
he likes to see confirmed, at least nominally, at the end.

All of this suggests that it is the author's divine mission to satisfy the greatest possible number of readers the
greatest possible number of times. It is a social duty, because,
after all, a book is not written in a vacuum, for the idle pleasure of its author . . .

This by way of _mise_ _en_ _scène_ for the shameful fact that
our end is already in our beginning--and middle. Throughout the
book we have adopted a sort of working attitude toward our subject, an attitude to which we have alluded with due frequency.
We early acknowledged the fact that our desire to apply language
analysis to literature was a problematical objective, one fraught
with all the perils of scrap-paper thinking. And we found that
certain language considerations furnished exemplary results when
applied to literature, while others worked less well.

Even at the end of the work, we don't feel confident saying that language analysis courses should be immediately added
to the standard literary criticism curriculum. While every critical theory has its stress points--areas in which it must be
slightly stretched out of shape in order to continue serving

as a useful pattern for the underlying sensuous material, we can't finally say that language analysis is in the forefront of the most stretchable. Aside from the almost definitional resemblance between language analysis and literature--that both display or use language in a conspicuous way--the aims of the two diverge almost completely from that point on.

In some ways this difference is an attractive advantage for the use of language analysis in literature. As a steel-cold diagnostic tool (at the most rigorous) this analysis avoids the stickiness that comes in the wake of two aesthetic bodies in contact. The creative shock of the unfamiliar can hardly be obtained from the juxtaposition of a florid critical essay and the lyric poem it purports to be about. The new and continuing interest in structuralism, for example, seems to be responding to the same kind of need, the desire to have a genuinely objective criterion for interpretation. Humanism's last words might be an invocation to the computer--'Arms and cybernetics I sing.' Which verse would of course be an undermining of electronics.

But digging deeper trenches is not our job here. We simply want to register the fact that literature these days is not content with the traditional analytic categories which grew originally out of the physical description of literature itself.

In a utopic world vision, there would at this moment be a firm knock at the door, followed by the sound of rending timber, after which the Figure of Language Analysis would come striding in, to raise Prostrate Literature to its feet and offer it a sturdy analytic elbow.

As this vision fades, we find ourselves facing the realities of the situation. It does not fall to our lot at the end of this work to calculate the worth of language analysis in itself. Because, 1) We had more or less accepted it on its own terms all along, and 2) We admittedly only dealt with those

aspects of it which we felt could help us in looking at literature. This of course leaves many virgin areas, and forestalls
any saturated study.

From the other side of the curtain, there were times in
this study when even those selected areas of language analysis
failed to meet head on the texts under consideration. Perhaps
it was the fault of the technique--the simple superposition of
these analytic indices onto a very different aesthetic.

This sort of telescoping may not be the ideal method.
Karl D. Uitti, for example, suggests a different approach which
is more bilateral:

> A possible starting point would be to divide, for
> purposes of analysis, literary "language" into
> two functions: a "rhetorical" and "stylistic"
> function or point of view that would permit the
> student to approach the text in terms of specif-
> ically aesthetic devices . . . and a general
> "linguistic" function (semiotic) that would allow
> the text in all its complexity to be incorporated
> into a body of material, techniques, and methods
> leading to a deeper understanding of sign
> mechanisms.[42]

Keeping these two areas of language separate might in practice
prove difficult. However, if the method is well-applied, it might
take the one-dimensionality out of literature which is undergoing "scientific" linguistic scrutiny.

Of course the point of view persists, that art, particularly
poetic art, is militantly special, that it cannot, without
really violating its own nature, subscribe to the ordinary laws
of discourse:

> Un langage "expressif" transmet de sujet à sujet,
> non seulement des informations, mais plus encore

---

[42]Karl D. Uitti, <u>Linguistics</u> and <u>Literary</u> <u>Theory</u>,
(Englewood Cliffs 1969), p. 191.

des sentiments, des attitudes, une vision des
choses. Aussi, il comporte toujours des
"déviations" par rapport aux règles d'une
sémantique et d'une syntaxe strictes: il se
forme une sémantique et même une syntaxe plus
appropriées à ses fins d'expression et de
suggestion.[43]

We have to lend this view of art at least half an ear,
since it is the rallying cry for a large population of writers,
readers, and critics. There is no doubt that art is special,
that it creates a particular and often rather private atmos-
phere with its stylistic and thematic devices. If one accepts
these devices, one enters, in effect, this aesthetic world; one
begins to live and think accordingly. And thought that is thus
modified by the art-object can't be the same thought that speaks
objectively and rationally about the art-object. Art, more
than most other objects creates and occupies an ontology which
is half its own, and half that of the life which gave it birth
and caused it to resemble life. Therefore, at the very moment
we are admitting art's hegemony we must also be struggling against
it, so the art-object does not extinguish our sun.

What we have achieved in this essay might be a journal of
that struggle, the record of life clashing against lifelike, the
bloodied track of mind fighting with almost-matter. If language
analysis can cause art to relent even a little, then there is
something to be said for this kind of thinking. If not, the
waters will close softly over the attempt, with few ripples.

---

[43]Noël Mouloud, Langage et structures, (Paris 1969), p.
71.

BIBLIOGRAPHY

Ayer, A. J. Language, Truth, and Logic. New York: Dover Pub-
lications, Inc., 1936.

Bens, Jacques. "Un langage-univers" in L'Écume des jours by
Boris Vian. Paris: Union Générale d'Éditions, 1963.

Booth, Wayne. The Rhetoric of Fiction. Chicago: University
of Chicago Press, 1961.

Carnap, Rudolf. The Logical Structure of the World & Pseudoprob-
lems in Philosophy. Berkeley: University of California
Press, 1967.

_____. Philosophy and Logical Syntax. London: Geo. Routledge
& Sons, Ltd., 1935.

Diderot, Denis. Paradoxe sur le comédien, in Oeuvres esthétiques.
Paris: Garnier, 1959.

Ducrot, Oswald. Qu'est-ce que le structuralisme? I. Le Structuralisme en linguistique. Paris: Éditions du seuil,
1968.

Fischer, Ernst. The Necessity of Art. Middlesex: Penguin Books,
1963.

Frege, Gottlob. "Über Sinn und Bedeutung." Zeitschrift für
Philosophie und philosophische Kritik, 100 (1892).

García Márquez, Gabriel. Cien años de soledad. Buenos Aires:
Editorial Sudamericana, 1969.

Greimas, A. J. Sémantique structurale. Paris: Larousse, 1966.

Imbert, Claude. G. Frege, Écrits logiques et philosophiques.
Paris: Éditions du Seuil, 1971.

Jakobson, Roman. Essais de linguistique générale. Paris: Éditions de minuit, 1963.

Lefebvre, Henri. Le langage et la société. Paris: Éditions
Gallimard, 1966.

Lenneberg, E. H. "A Biological Perspective of Language," in
Language, ed. R. C. Oldfield & J. C. Marshall. Middlesex:
Penguin Books, 1968.

Lledo, Emilio. Filosofía y lenguaje. Barcelona: Editorial
Ariel, 1974.

Marr, Nikolaus. "Über die Entstehung der Sprache," in Unter
dem Banner des Marxismus, 3 (1926).

Martínez Bonati, Félix. La estructura de la obra literaria.
Barcelona: Editorial Seix Barral, 1972.

Mouloud, Noël. Langage et structures. Paris: Payot, 1969.

Núñez Ladeveze, Luis. Crítica del discurso literario. Madrid:
Cuadernos para el diálogo, 1974.

Pears, David. Wittgenstein. London: Fontana, 1971.

Pope, Alexander, Poetry and Prose, ed. Aubrey Williams. Boston:
Houghton Mifflin Company, 1969.

Romains, Jules. Knock. Paris: Éditions Gallimard, 1924.

Russell, Bertrand. Human Knowledge: Its Scope and Limits.
New York: Humanities Press Inc., 1948.

_____. Introduction to Mathematical Philosophy. London:
George Allen & Unwin, Ltd., 1919.

Ryle, Gilbert. The Concept of Mind. New York: Barnes & Noble,
1949.

Structuralisme et marxisme. Paris: Union Générale d'Éditions,
1970.

Uitti, Karl D. Linguistics and Literary Theory. Englewood Cliffs:
Prentice Hall, 1969.

Ullmo, Jean. La Pensée scientifique moderne. Paris: Flammarion,
1969.

Wellek, René & Warren, Austin. Theory of Literature. New York:
Harcourt, Brace & World, Inc., 1956.

Whorf, Benjamin Lee. Language, Thought and Reality. Cambridge:
The M.I.T. Press, 1956.

Wittgenstein, Ludwig. _Philosophical Investigations_. Oxford:
    Basil Blackwell, 1953.

_____. _Tractatus Logico-Philosophicus_. London: Routledge
    & Kegan Paul, 1961.

Poetic Diction in Ben Jonson. ELSIE LEACH: T. S. Eliot and the School of Donne. SEYMOUR REITER: The Structure of 'Waiting for Godot'. DANIEL E. VAN TASSEL: The Search for Manhood in D. H. Lawrence's 'Sons and Lovers'. MARVIN ROSENBERG: Poetry of the Theatre. GUY R. WOOD-ALL: James Russell Lowell's "Works of Jeremy Taylor, D.D.'

Volume 4. Amsterdam 1972. 233 p. Hfl. 40.–
BOGDDY ARIAS: Sailor's Reveries. R. H. BOWERS: Marlowe's 'Dr. Faustus', Tirso's 'El Condenado por Desconfiado', and the Secret Cause. HOWARD O. BROGAN: Satirist Burns and Lord Byron. WELLER EMBLER: Simone Weil and T. S. Eliot. E. ANTHONY JAMES: Defoe's Autobiographical Apologia: Rhetorical Slanting in 'An Appeal to Honour and Justice'. MARY D. KRAMER: The American Wild West Show and "Buffalo Bill" Cody. IRVING MASSEY: Shelley's "Dirge for the Year": The Relation of the Holograph to the First Edition. L. J. MORRISSEY: English Street Theatre: 1655–1708. M. PATRICK: Browning's Dramatic Techniques and 'The Ring and the Book': A Study in Mechanic and Organic Unity. VINCENT F. PETRONELLA: Shakespeare's 'Henry V' and the Second Tetralogy: Meditation as Drama. NASEEB SHAHEEN: Deriving Adjectives from Nouns. TED R. SPIVEY: The Apocalyptic Symbolism of W. B. Yeats and T. S. Eliot. EDWARD STONE: The Other Sermon in 'Moby–Dick'. M. G. WILLIAMS: 'In Memoriam': A Broad Church Poem.

Volume 5. Amsterdam 1972. 236 p. Hfl. 40.–
PETER G. BEIDLER: Chaucer's Merchant and the Tale of January. ROBERT A. BRYAN: Poets, Poetry, and Mercury in Spenser's Prosopopia: Mother Hubberd's Tale. EDWARD M. HOLMES: Requiem For A Scarlet Nun. E. ANTHONY JAMES: Defoe's Narrative Artistry: Naming and Describing in Robinson Crusoe. MICHAEL J. KELLY: Coleridge's "Picture, or The Lover's Resolution": its Relationship to "Dejection" and its Sources in the Notebooks. EDWARD MARGOLIES: The Playwright and his Critics. MURRAY F. MARKLAND: The Task Set by Valor. RAYMOND S. NELSON: Back to Methuselah: Shaw's Modern Bible. THOMAS W. ROSS: Maimed Rites in Much Ado About Nothing. WILLIAM B. TOOLE: The Metaphor of Alchemy in Julius Caesar. PAUL WEST: Carlyle's Bravura Prophetics. GLENA D. WOOD: The Tragi-Comic Dimensions of Lear's Fool. H. ALAN WYCHER-LEY: "Americana": The Mencken – Lorimer Feud.

Volume 6. Amsterdam 1972. 235 p. Hfl. 40.–
GEORG W. BOSWELL: Superstition and Belief in Faulkner. ALBERT COOK: Blake's Milton. MARSHA KINDER: The Improved Author's Farce: An Analysis of the 1734 Revisions. ABE LAUFE: What Makes Drama Run? (Introduction to Anatomy of a Hit). RICHARD L. LOUGHLIN: Laugh and Grow Wise with Oliver Goldsmith. EDWARD MARGOLIES: The American Detective Thriller & The Idea of Society. RAYMOND S. NELSON: Shaw's Heaven, Hell, and Redemption. HAROLD OREL: Is Patrick White's Voss the Real Leichhardt of Australia? LOUIS B. SALOMON: A Walk With Emerson On The Dark Side. H. GRANT SAMPSON: Structure in the Poetry of Thoreau. JAMES H. SIMS, Some Biblical Light on Shakespeare's Hamlet.

ROBERT F. WILLSON, Jr.: Lear's Auction. JAMES N. WISE: Emerson's "Experience" and "Sons and Lovers". JAMES D. YOUNG: Aims in Reader's Theatre.

Volume 7. Amsterdam 1973. 235 p. Hfl. 40.—
HANEY H. BELL Jr.: Sam Fathers and Ike McCaslin and the World in Which Ike Matures. SAMUEL IRVING BELLMAN: The Apocalypse in Literature. HALDEEN BRADDY: England and English before Alfred. DAVID R. CLARK: Robert Frost: "The Thatch" and "Directive". RALPH MAUD: Robert Crowley, Puritan Satirist. KATHARINE M. MORSBERGER: Hawthorne's "Borderland": The Locale of the Romance. ROBERT E. MORSBERGER: The Conspiracy of the Third International. "What is the metre of the dictionary?" – Dylan Thomas. RAYMOND PRESTON: Dr. Johnson and Aristotle. JOHN J. SEYDOW: The Sound of Passing Music: John Neal's Battle for American Literary Independence. JAMES H. SIMS: Enter Satan as Esau, Alone; Exit Satan as Belshazzar: *Paradise Lost*, BOOK (IV). MICHAEL WEST, Dryden and the Disintegration of Renaissance Heroic Ideals. RENATE C. WOLFF: Pamela as Myth and Dream.

Volume 8. Amsterdam 1973. 231 p. Hfl. 40.—
SAMUEL I. BELLMAN: Sleep, Pride, and Fantasy: Birth Traumas and Socio-Biologic Adaptation in the American-Jewish Novel. PETER BUITEN-HUIS: A Corresponding Fabric: The Urban World of Saul Bellow. DAVID R. CLARK: An Excursus upon the Criticism of Robert Frost's "Directive". FRANCIS GILLEN: Tennyson and the Human Norm: A Study of Hubris and Human Commitment in Three Poems by Tennyson. ROBERT R. HARSON: H. G. Wells: The Mordet Island Episode. JULIE B. KLEIN: The Art of Apology: "An Epistle to Dr. Arbuthnot" and "Verses on the Death of Dr. Swift". ROBERT E. MORSBERGER: The Movie Game in Who's Afraid of Virginia Woolf and The Boys in the Band. EDWIN MOSES: A Reading of "The Ancient Mariner". JOHN H. RANDALL: Romeo and Juliet in the New World. A Study in James, Wharton, and Fitzgerald "Fay ce que vouldras". JOHN E. SAVESON: Conrad as Moralist in Victory. ROBERT M. STROZIER: Politics, Stoicism, and the Development of Elizabethan Tragedy. LEWIS TURCO: Manoah Bodman: Poet of the Second Awakening.

Volume 9. Amsterdam 1973. 251 p. Hfl. 40.—
THOMAS E. BARDEN: Dryden's Aims in *Amphytryon*. SAMUEL IRVING BELLMAN: Marjorie Kinnan Rawling's Existentialist Nightmare *The Yearling*. SAMUEL IRVING BELLMAN: Writing Literature for Young People. Marjorie Kinnan Rawlings' "Secret River" of the Imagination. F. S. JANZOW: "Philadelphus," A New Essay by De Quincey. JACQUELINE KRUMP: Robert Browning's Palace of Art. ROBERT E. MORSBERGER: The Winning of Barbara Undershaft: Conversion by the Cannon Factory, or "Wot prawce selvytion nah?" DOUGLAS L. PETERSON: Tempest-Tossed Barks and Their Helmsmen in Several of Shakespeare's Plays. STANLEY POSS: Serial Form and Malamud's Schlemihls. SHERYL P. RUTLEDGE: Chaucer's Zodiac of Tales. CONSTANCE RUYS: John Pickering—Merchant Adventurer and Playwright. JAMES H. SIMS: Death in Poe's Poetry: Varia-

tions on a Theme. ROBERT A. SMITH: A Pioneer Black Writer and the Problems of Discrimination and Miscegenation. ALBERT J. SOLOMON: The Sound of Music in "Eveline": A Long Note on a Barrel-Organ. J. L. STYAN: Goldsmith's Comic Skills. ARLINE R. THORN: Shelley's *The Cenci* as Tragedy. E. THORN: James Joyce: Early Imitations of Structural Unity. LEWIS TURCO: The Poetry of Lewis Turco. An Interview by Gregory Fitzgerald and William Heyen.

New Series. Volume 1. Edited by James L. W. West III. Amsterdam 1974. 194 p. Hfl. 40.—
D. W. ROBERTSON, Jr.: Chaucer's Franklin and His Tale. CLARENCE H. MILLER and CARYL K. BERREY: The Structure of Integrity: The Cardinal Virtues in Donne's "Satyre III". F. SAMUEL JANZOW: The English Opium-Eater as Editor. VICTOR A. KRAMER: Premonition of Disaster: An Unpublished Section for Agee's *A Death in the Family*. GEORGE L. GECKLE: Poetic Justice and *Measure for Measure*. RODGER L. TARR: Thomas Carlyle's Growing Radicalism: The Social Context of *The French Revolution*. G. THOMAS TANSELLE: Philip Gaskell's *A New Introduction to Bibliography*. Review Essay. KATHERINE B. TROWER: Elizabeth D. Kirk's *The Dream Thought of Piers Plowman*. Review Essay. JAMES L. WEST III: Matthew J. Bruccoli's *F. Scott Fitzgerald a Descriptive Bibliography*. Review Essay. JAMES E. KIBLER: R. W. Stallman's *Stephen Crane: A Critical Bibliography*. Review. ROBERT P. MILLER: Jonathan Saville's *The Medieval Erotic Alba*. Review.

New Series. Volume 2. **THACKERY**. **Edited by Peter L. Shillingsburg**. Amsterdam 1974. 359 p. Hfl. 70.—
JOAN STEVENS: *Vanity Fair* and the London Skyline. JANE MILLGATE: History *versus* Fiction: Thackeray's Response to Macaulay. ANTHEA TRODD: Michael Angelo Titmarsh and the Knebworth Apollo. PATRICIA R. SWEENEY: Thackeray's Best Illustrator. JOAN STEVENS: Thackeray's Pictorial Capitals. ANTHONY BURTON: Thackeray's Collaborations with Cruikshank, Doyle, and Walker. JOHN SUTHERLAND: A *Vanity Fair* Mystery: The Delay in Publication. JOHN SUTHERLAND: Thackeray's Notebook for *Henry Esmond*. EDGAR F. HARDEN: The Growth of *The Virginians* as a Serial Novel: Parts 1—9. GERALD C. SORENSEN: Thackeray Texts and Bibliographical Scholarship. PETER L. SHILLINSBURG: Thackeray Texts: A Guide to Inexpensive Editions. RUTH apROBERTS: Thackeray Boom: A Review. JOSEPH E. BAKER: Reading Masterpieces in Isolation: Review. ROBERT A. COLBY and JOHN SUTHERLAND: Thackeray's Manuscripts: A Preliminary Census of Library Locations.

New Series. Volume 3. Edited by James L. W. West III. Amsterdam 1975. 184 p. Hfl. 40.—
SAMUEL J. ROGAL: Hurd's Editorial Criticism of Addison's Grammar and Usage. ROBERT P. MILLER: Constancy Humanized: Trivet's Constance and the Man of Law's Custance. WELDON THORNTON: Structure and Theme in Faulkner's *Go Down, Moses*. JAYNE K. KRIBBS: John Davis: A Man For His Time. STEPHEN E. MEATS: The Responsibilities of an Editor of Correspon-

dence. Review Essay. RODGER L. TARR: Carlyle and Dickens *or* Dickens and Carlyle. Review. CHAUNCEY WOOD: Courtly Lovers: An Unsentimental View. Review.

New Series. Volume 4. Edited by James L. W. West III. Amsterdam 1975. 179 p. Hfl. 40.–
JAMES L. W. WEST III: A Bibliographer's Interview with William Styron. J. TIMOTHY HOBBS: The Doctrine of Fair Use in the Law of Copyright. JUNE STEFFENSEN HAGEN: Tennyson's Revisions of the Last Stanza of "Audley Court". CLIFFORD CHALMERS HUFFMAN: *The Christmas Prince*: University and Popular Drama in the Age of Shakespeare. ROBERT L. OAKMAN: Textual Editing and the Computer. Review Essay. T.H. HOWARD-HILL: The Bard in Chains: *The Harvard Concordance to Shakespeare*. Review Essay. BRUCE HARKNESS: Conrad Computerized and Concordanced. Review Essay. MIRIAM J. SHILLINGSBURG: A Rose is a Four-Letter Word; or, The Machine Makes Another Concordance. Review Essay. RICHARD H. DAMMERS: Explicit Statement as Art. Review Essay. A. S. G. EDWARDS: Medieval Madness and Medieval Literature. Review Essay. NOEL POLK: Blotner's Faulkner. Review.

New Series. Volume 5–6. **GYASCUTUS. Studies in Antebellum Southern Humorous and Sporting Writing. Edited by James L. W. West III.** Amsterdam 1978.
NOEL POLK: The Blind Bull, Human Nature: Sut Lovingood and the Damned Human Race. HERBERT P. SHIPPEY: William Tappan Thompson as Playwright. LELAND H. COX, Jr.: Porter's Edition of *Instructions to Young Sportsmen*. ALAN GRIBBEN: Mark Twain Reads Longstreet's *Georgia Scenes*. T. B. THORPE's Far West Letters, ed. Leland H. Cox, Jr. An Unknown Tale by GEORGE WASHINGTON HARRIS ed. William Starr. JOHNSON JONES HOOPER's "The 'Frinnolygist' at Fault" ed. James L. W. West III. SOUTH CAROLINA WRITERS in the *Spirit of the Times* ed. Stephen E. Meats. A NEW MOCK SERMON ed. James L. W. West III. ANOTHER NEW MOCK SERMON ed. A. S. Wendel. The PORTER-HOOPER Correspondence ed. Edgar E. Thompson.

New Series. Volume 7. **SANFORD PINSKER: The Languages of Joseph Conrad.** Amsterdam 1978. 87 p. Hfl. 20.–
Table of Contents: Foreword. Introductory Language. The Language of the East. The Language of Narration. The Language of the Sea. The Language of Politics. *Victory* As Afterword.

New Series. Volume 8. **GARLAND CANNON: An Integrated Transformational Grammar of the English Language.** Amsterdam 1978. 315 p. Hfl. 60.–
Table of Contents: Preface. 1) A Child's Acquisition of His First Language. 2) Man's Use of Language. 3) Syntactic Component: Base Rules. 4) Syntactic Component: Lexicon. 5) Syntactic Component: Transformational Rules. 6) Semantic Component. 7) Phonological Component. 8) Man's Understanding of His Language. Appendix: the Sentence-Making Model. Bibliography. Index.

New Series: Volume 9. **GERALD LEVIN: Richardson the Novelist: The Psychological Patterns.** Amsterdam 1978. 172 p. Hfl. 30.—
Table of Contents: Preface. Chapter One. The Problem of Criticism. Chapter Two. "Conflicting Trends" in *Pamela.* Chapter Three. Lovelace's Dream. Chapter Four. The "Family Romance" of *Sir Charles Grandison.* Chapter Five. Richardson's Art. Chapter Six. Richardson and Lawrence: the Rhetoric of Concealment. Appendix. Freud's Theory of Masochism. Bibliography.

New Series: Volume 10. **WILLIAM F. HUTMACHER: Wynkyn de Worde and Chaucer's Canterbury Tales. A Transcription and Collation of the 1498 Edition with Caxton[2] from the General Prologue Through the Knights Tale.** Amsterdam 1978. 224 p. Hfl. 40,—
Table of Contents: Introduction. Wynkyn's Life and Works. Wynkyn De Word's Contribution to Printing. Significance of Wynkyn's *The Canterbury Tales.* Significance of Wynkyn's Order of the Tales. Scheme of the Order of *·The Canterbury Tales.* Wynkyn's Variants from CX[2]. Printer's Errors. Spelling. Omissions in Wynkyn's Edition. Additions in Wynkyn's Edition. Transpositions in Wynkyn's Edition. Miscellaneous Variants in the Reading. Bibliography. Explanation of the Scheme of the Transcription and Recording of the Variants. The Transcription and Collation.

New Series: Volume 11. **WILLIAM R. KLINK: S. N. Behrman: The Major Plays.** Amsterdam 1978. 272 p. Hfl. 45,—
Table of Contents: Introduction. *The Second Man. Brief Moment. Biography. Rain From Heaven. End of Summer. No Time for Comedy. The Talley Method. But For Whom Charlie.* Language. Conclusion. Bibliography.

New Series: Volume 12. **VALERIE BONITA GRAY:** *Invisible Man's* Literary heritage: *Benito Cereno* and *Moby Dick.* Amsterdam 1978. 145p. Hfl. 30,—
Table of Contents: Democracy: The Politics of "Affirming the Principle" and Celebrating the Individual. The Spectrum of Ambiguity: From Mask Wearing to Shape-shifting. Whiteness or Blackness: Which Casts the Shadow? Melville's and Ellison's Methodology: Bird Imagery and Whale and Circus Lore. Social Protest. Bibliography.

New Series: Volume 13. **VINCENT DIMARCO and LESLIE PERELMAN: The Middle English Letter of Alexander to Aristotle.** Amsterdam 1978. 194p. Hfl. 40,—

New Series: Volume 14. **JOHN W. CRAWFORD: Discourse: Essays on English and American Literature.** Amsterdam 1978. 200p. 40,—
Contents: Chaucer's Use of Sun Imagery. The Fire from Spenser's Dragon: "The Faerie Queene," I.xi. The Changing Renaissance World in Thomas Deloney's Fiction. Shakespeare's Falstaff: A Thrust at Platonism. The Religious Question in *Julius Caesar.* Teaching *Julius Caesar:* A Study in Poetic Persuasion. Shakespeare: A Lesson in Communications. Intuitive Knowledge in *Cymbeline.* White Witchcraft in Tudor-Stuart Drama. Another

Biblical Allusion in *Paradise Lost*. *Absalom and Achitophel;* and Milton's *Paradise Lost*. Asem-Goldsmith's Solution to Timon's Dilemma. Dr. Johnson: A Modern Example of Christian Constancy. A Unifying Element in Tennyson's *Maud*. Arnold's Relevancy to the Twentieth Century. Sophocles' Role in "Dover Beach". Lest We Forget, Lest We Forget: Kipling's Warning to Humanity. The Garden Imagery in *Great Expectations*. "Victorian" Women in *Barchester Towers*. Another Look at "Youth". Forster's "The Road from Colonus". Biblical Influences in *Cry, the Beloved Country*. Huxley's *Island:* A Contemporary *Utopia*. The Generation Gap in Literature. Bred and Bawn in a Briar Patch — Deception in the Making. Success and Failure in the Poetry of Edwin Arlington Robinson. Naturalistic Tendencies in *Spoon River Anthology*. Primitiveness in "The Bravest Boat". Theme of Suffering in "Sonny's Blues". Nabokov's "First Love". The Temper of Romanticism in *Travels with Charley*. Unrecognized Artists in American Literature: Chicano Renaissance.

New Series: Volume 15. **ROBERT F. WILLSON, JR.: Landmarks of Shakespeare Criticism.** Amsterdam 1979. 113p. 25,—
Contents: Introduction. Thomas Rymer: On *Othello* (1692). Nicholas Rowe: Preface (1709-14). Alexander Pope: Preface (1725). Lewis Theobald: Preface (1740). Samuel Johnson: Preface (1765). Richard Farmer: Essay on the Learning of Shakespeare (1767). Gotthold Lessing: On Ghosts (1769). Walter Whiter: On Hell and Night in *Macbeth* (1794). William Richardson: On the Faults of Shakespeare (1797). August Wilhelm von Schlegel: Lecture XXIII. Shakespeare (1809-11). Johann Wolfgang von Goethe: Shakespeare ad Infinitum (1812?). Samuel Taylor Coleridge: On Shakespeare as a Poet (1811-12). William Hazlitt: On Shakespeare and Milton (1818). Thomas de Quincey: On the Knocking at the Gate in *Macbeth* (1823). Thomas Carlyle: The Hero as a Poet (1841). Ivan Turgenev: Hamlet and Don Quixote: the Two Eternal Human Types (1860). Edward Dowden: Shakespeare's Portraiture of Women (1888). Walter Pater: Shakespeare's English Kings (1889). Bernard ten Brink: Shakespeare as a Comic Poet (1895). Richard Moulton: Supernatural Agency in the Moral World of Shakespeare (1903). Leo Tolstoy: Shakespeare and the Drama (1906). J.J. Jusserand: What to Expect of Shakespeare (1911-12). Sigmund Freud: On Lady Macbeth (1916). George Bernard Shaw: On Cutting Shakespear (1919). Edmund Blunden: Shakespeare's Significances (1929). Selected Bibliography.

New Series: Volume 16. **A.H. Qureshi: Edinburgh Review and Poetic Truth.** Amsterdam 1979. 61p. 15,—

New Series: Volume 17. **RAYMOND J.S. GRANT: Cambridge Corpus Christi College 41: The Loricas and the Missal.** Amsterdam 1979. 127p. 30,—
Contents: Chapter I: The Loricas of Corpus 41. Chapter II: Corpus 41 — An 11th-Century English Missal. Appendix: Latin Liturgical material contained in

the Margins of Cambridge, Corpus Christi College 41. Endnotes: Chapter I and Chapter II.

Editions Rodopi N.V., Keizersgracht 302-304, Amsterdam, the Netherlands.